Effective Management Techniques for Getting Things Done

by
Lynn W. Whiteside

PARKER PUBLISHING COMPANY, INC.
WEST NYACK, N.Y.

PRINTED IN THE UNITED STATES OF AMERICA
B & P

The author wishes to thank Mrs. Jean E. Overeem for her special efforts and encouragement in the preparation of the manuscript—for her typing, proofreading, and valuable suggestions.

What This Book Can Do for You

Effective Management Techniques for Getting Things Done is a successful approach to combining management skills with forward-looking attitudes in achieving your goals as a business manager. The system shows you how to direct, guide, and assist employees to get outstanding results. In this book you will find personally observed, on-the-job problems and a description of how they were handled. You can evaluate your own performance by comparing your management actions against these examples.

In examining the uses of the system, you'll discover how to become more effective in your profession. You'll learn how to build a solid stance, how to let important people know that you are around, and how to stretch yourself to win a better position in the difficult and fascinating art of directing others. The many guidelines for action will be of great value, not only in employee relations but also in showing the way to self-improvement in specific managerial skills.

Effective Management Techniques will supply just the tool that you need to move rapidly upward in management.

The system began to develop while I was experiencing a wide variety of problems as a manager at many levels. During my years as a supervisor, foreman, and plant superintendent in the headquarters organization of the Goodyear Tire and Rubber Company and the Goodyear Aircraft Corporation, I was exposed to numerous episodes of both good and bad judgment. This study of the difficult profession of management continued when I began creating and directing an extensive management development effort for The Boeing Company.

Effective Management Techniques is the crystallization of these years of study and experience. It explains in practical terms the lessons learned.

The first four chapters, Part I, tell HOW TO BUILD A BASE FOR SUCCESS IN MANAGEMENT.

In the opening chapter are examples which alert you to what other people most frequently respond to, based on generally held desires and convictions.

Chapter 2 reveals how this opportunity system helps you to better handle your resources.

You can use the ideas in Chapter 3 to avoid management mistakes and to more effectively apply judgment decisions.

Chapter 4 shows you how to get needed results without arousing resentment. You'll also learn how to be a "stay-alive" manager.

In the next four chapters, Part II, you will discover HOW TO HANDLE YOUR PRESENT JOB TO ADVERTISE YOUR ABILITY.

How to get more performance per dollar spent, some profit pointers, and ways to get greater mileage from available money, supply special value to Chapter 5.

The stimulating exercises in Chapter 6 provide proven, original approaches to make you a standout in productive job creation.

Chapter 7 gives reality to demand, supply, and price. A better understanding of these essentials will shortcut your problems.

How to be more competitive, the central thread of Chapter 8, will aid your progress to the top and reinforce your staying power.

In the last four chapters, Part III, you will learn HOW YOU CAN STEP UP TO A HIGHER JOB WITH YOUR BEST PER-FORMANCE.

Chapter 9 frames the "big picture" and helps you follow the right guidelines on your upward progress.

General business ups and downs with look-ahead management in Chapter 10 spell out where to find useful information and how to read it, with a "How-am-I-doing?" test.

Five management keys for promoting prosperity provide get-results essentials for checking your performance in Chapter 11.

The final chapter helps you meet others' security desires while carrying through your total responsibility.

Effective Management Techniques for Getting Things Done will open a broad, inviting highway and help you travel it to a top-executive management position in the business of your choice.

Contents

vii

Part II

HANDLE YOUR PRESENT JOB TO ADVERTISE YOUR ABILITY

Part III

STEP UP TO A MORE RESPONSIBLE JOB BY STRETCHING YOUR PERFORMANCE TO MEET YOUR POTENTIAL

I

BUILD A SOLID BASE FOR
YOUR SUCCESS AS A MANAGER

1

How to Manage to Get
What You Want

To build a base for your progress as an effective manager, you must fully commit yourself to professionalizing your conduct in all facets of this demanding job. You must have more than your share of determination not to be stopped. Always remember that self-dedication is a key ingredient.

You must develop these qualities on your own because, "...it makes relatively little difference to a business firm whether its junior executives are motivated toward advancement by vanity, by keeping up with the Joneses, by lust for authority, by a miserly desire to accumulate wealth, or by a dedication to the interests of the business firm." [1]

The point is that you must acquire this *drive to succeed* as a foundation for building your leadership in the organization you serve.

How to Use Effective Management Techniques

The many techniques described in this book constitute a method of effective management, evolved during years of business experience, which combine the two most essential skills every successful manager must acquire: practical skill in dealing with people and problems, and personal skill in maintaining positive attitudes about yourself and your work.

The first thing to remember is that you must keep striving. One of history's most renowned managers ran the gamut of failures before he reached his goal as one of the nation's greatest leaders. For instance, in 1831 he failed in business. The next year, he was defeated in a try for a seat in the state legislature. Another attempt at business failed in 1833. He succeeded in being elected to the legislature in 1834. After trying and failing to be elected to Congress in 1843, he achieved success in 1846. However, he was defeated for re-election to the very next Congress in 1848. Later, he tried and was defeated for the Senate in 1855. In 1858, he again failed in an effort to become a Senator.

Yet, Abraham Lincoln didn't quit in spite of experiencing just enough successes to make the losses more painful. His failures are forgotten; and he is remembered as a winner, an on-top manager.

Lincoln's determination enabled him to work this flexible system for a position on the pinnacle of leadership. This same course is open to you if you understand and fully use your position, chances, and prospects for advancement.

Regardless of the name which may be attached to the system under which you as a manager must operate, realistically it boils down to what you as one of the select group of leaders make it. This is the strength and opportunity of the system. As you strive to become a better manager, emphasize *people-results* in your thinking and working. You may lay out a perfect assembly line, develop wonderful materials, and figure out the greatest mathematical formulas, but if people fail to respond favorably to your direction you're not a successful manager.

This makes attention to people a first priority for building your success base in management.

Understand Human Nature Better

Thus it's up to you to know as much as possible about people and what causes them to do the things they do. The economist, Adam Smith, wrote in 1776, "Each individual seeks to employ his capital so that its produce may be of greatest value. He generally neither intends to promote the public interest, nor knows how much he is promoting it." Continuing, this great thinker surmised that while each person selfishly looked *first* to his own interest, very often this attention to his own security and gain contributed more to the betterment of society than his actions would if he deliberately set out to be a do-gooder for others. To make the most of the system, you must use it for your own personal advantage. You must not miss any opportunity to further your self-development.

How to Use the Desires of People

Abraham Lincoln knew what he wanted from his career. This suggests one of the ways that many managers handicap themselves when they fail to appreciate the variety of things which individuals consider important.

To make this idea useful, your approach must be to:

1. Determine what you are trying to accomplish.

2. Remind yourself that all the people with whom you work have desires important to them, even though they might appear of picayunish significance to you.

    a. Your union steward wants a grievance answered because his personal prestige with the people he represents and with his organizational superior is involved.

    b.   An employee wants to go fishing with his son on a special day.

    c.   The industrial engineer wants to build his personal reputation by having you meet the schedule he has set.

    d.   The inspector is concerned with your quality because excellence of output is first in his book.

    e.   The cost control specialist watches your expense curve with high hopes that it will further his special interests.

    f.   Don't overlook the fact that the person you report to wants to be known as a knowledgeable manager.

3.   Find out the specific wants of those with whom you must work.

4.   Make these desires a part of your repertory of management tools to be used with vigor and judgment to further your own progress toward your selected goal.

How to Avoid an Explosion

When you follow this four-point formula, you are getting into position to prevent real trouble.

While some complaining is normal, you can't afford to neglect the signs of major difficulty. Thus, the better you are informed about what others want, the more opportunities you have to head off real problems. As an assist to your thinking, remember that others, as well as yourself, are continually asking the question (maybe not out loud, but real, nevertheless), "What's in it for me?"

Check your own strongest urge. Do you endeavor to excel in your job because: (1) You like it? (2) You like the money you make? (3) It enables you to feel important? (4) You are doing something few people can do?

Whatever you checked, there are certain, selected, minimum needs which, if unsatisfied, are a warning barometer of coming trouble. Generally applied to managers, they are: (1) You must see a better future. (2) You must be paid what you consider a fair wage for what you do. (3) You must receive some status symbols important to you. These may be badges, carpets on the floor, offices, secretaries, parking privileges. (4) You must have some sense of professional job security.

How to Look at Your Improvement Effort

Since this system is linked with Adam Smith's basic philosophy, as a manager you can increase your skills, improve your performance, and move ahead in your profession by gaining and using know-how about this unique management formula.

1. Look at and study how you can profit from the network of inter-twined people-economic relationships which form the base to help you on your way.
2. Seize at-hand occasions to advertise your performance abilities.
3. Push yourself. Exercise the outer limits of your developed skills and talents.

As you work to build a base for your success as a manager, be sure: (1) to know the effects of history, culture, and climate on your industry; (2) to determine the economic support of your area; (3) to find out as much as possible about the people with whom you live and associate. Such information will help you be a leader in your company——which is required of a successful manager.

However, to really make a solid base for your management success, you must have the assistance of your superiors, your associates, and your subordinates. Some actions you can take in this direction are to encourage the growth of those reporting to you.

How You Can Help Subordinates Do a Better Job

When electronic data processing equipment and methods became available in a large manufacturing plant, several departments set up their own groups to provide needed services. Engineering concentrated on scientific information; Industrial Relations on employee problems; Manufacturing on scheduling details; and Finance determined costs, payrolls, and sales data. Each of these functions was important, and over a period of several years well-staffed units were established in these four departments.

When equipment costs started mounting, division manager Al Cook directed plant industrial engineering department director John Stephan to advise him on what should be done to accomplish cost-savings in the data processing operation.

John was back in Al's office the next day with the complaint that his men found it impossible to get the cooperation they needed to carry out the assignment. The division manager listened and then asked, "Do you want me to get someone else to do the job?" The industrial engineer quickly understood the message and assured the boss that he could handle the problem.

John and his staff compiled a list of questions about amounts, quality, and frequency of use of computers. In addition, all objections to a centralized unit were solicited from the four departments.

After all this information had been accumulated, John took it in to Al's office to talk with him about it. As the engineer started relating the details, Al asked, "What's your recommendation?" It then dawned upon John that he still had work to do, so he hurriedly excused himself.

When John later came back to the general manager's office, he recommended that a central data processing unit be set up, reporting to an assistant general manager. This unit was to provide all computer services for the entire plant. The engineer had supporting details for his suggestions. Al looked this over briefly and commended John for a thorough coverage of the assignment.

After consultation with the several department heads, John's recommendations were adopted. Savings went well over $2 million a year; and, when pressed, the using departments admitted that services had improved.

In building a base for your progress as a professional manager, one of the key factors is growth by those reporting to you. This can be accomplished by:

1. Encouraging subordinates to take personal responsibility and exercise judgment;
2. Helping them to collect and evaluate facts;
3. Adding to their understanding of human nature;
4. Giving subordinates a working charter for more effectively handling assigned work; and
5. Letting them experience the personal satisfaction of carrying through an important piece of work.

As you manage to get what you want, keeping your subordinates' loyalty is vital to your success.

How You Can Meet the Output Needs of Those Reporting to You

In the presence of national, state, and city government officials, special guests, plant officials, and newsmen, the thousandth all-aluminum railroad passenger car was rolled from the assembly plant.

Interest in this event was prompted by a spontaneously generous gesture taken by employees to further the March of Dimes fund drive. In the plant, as soon as the first sizable assembly of the thousandth car was completed, someone taped money to the structure with a notice of its purpose. The idea caught on and other shops and groups followed with coins and bills.

For the employees, this thousandth car had an additional attraction because it marked two years of uninterrupted, on-schedule production without a major rework.

What does the thousandth railroad car ceremony have to do with your building a solid base for management success? It should remind you that most employees want to:

1. Contribute to the worthwhile output of your company,
2. Do an outstanding job,
3. Feel good about a successful team effort,
4. Have an opportunity to express their generosity, and
5. Get public recognition.

As you meet the wants and needs of the people under your direction, you are taking a long step toward earning their loyal cooperation.

How Effective Management Techniques Encourage Efficiency

Closely related to an employee's output need is his distaste for waste. Longtime records show that on the average, when there is the possibility of a personal reward, better than one out of every three employees will suggest at least one method, machine, or other efficiency improvement each year. A real drive for new ideas will step this participation up to an average of one suggestion for every two employees.

This tells you several things valuable to you as a manager:

1. Workmen want to see operations performed in the easiest and best way.

2. A sizable percentage of employees think about how their jobs might be more efficiently handled.

3. These more intelligent workmen recognize that progress is inevitable.

4. Immediate rewards are powerful motivators.

How to Use the Family-Pride Urge in Your Managing

As you endeavor to build a strong base for your success in management, remember that the people who look to you for leadership have strong family ties.

In the finance department of a large retail store, Mrs. Smith worked as a business machine operator. Her son Frank was a standout high school athlete and a superior student.

At times, Dave Johnson (the supervisor of the finance department) became a little weary of hearing about Frank's exploits from his mother. Mrs. Smith frequently selected the time in which Dave wanted to relax for relating what her son had achieved. This is not a simple problem, so ask yourself what you would do. Would you: (a) Explain to her that you needed some free time? (b) Point out that she was not the only mother who wanted to talk about her son? (c) Transfer her to another department? (d) Assign more work for her? Here's what Dave did. He weighed the fact that Mrs. Smith was:

1. A very productive and hard-working employee.

2. Helpful by willingly adjusting her schedule to work overtime when necessary.

3. Never absent or late.

4. Able to work well with everyone in the office.

5. Especially good at training new employees.

6. Quick to recognize when Dave was really busy and not bother him with her personal affairs at these times.

As an ambitious manager, Dave concluded that an employee with all these pluses deserved to have a friendly, sincerely interested listener when she wanted to talk about her son. In fact, the finance department manager was told by his boss that Mrs. Smith, under another earlier manager, was a problem employee. So Dave wisely concluded that his attention to her interests played a major role in changing her attitude.

Another part of this significant episode was that Frank's father, a highly skilled lathe operator for the Triple A Company, a small tool shop, was considering changing jobs by moving to a larger shop with fewer changes and a smoother flow of work. Alfred Sturn, the owner-manager of the Triple A, found that paying equal wages with competing firms failed to hold the employees he needed. In his conversations with Mr. Smith, Alfred learned that Frank was ambitious to become a mechanical engineer.

This led Mr. Sturn to suggest that Frank might like a part-time job for experience and, if things went along satisfactorily, he could continue full-time work for the summer. The shop owner also proposed to Mr. Smith that his alma mater would be happy to admit Frank as a student.

Applying effective management techniques Alfred not only helped the father and son but also was able to benefit from opportunities to use the natural, human pride-in-family urge as an influencer of people important to his future in management.

How to Apply Wage Demands for More Effective Management

In a further exploration of the things which get favorable responses from others, note that most people want to feel they earn what they receive. The wage a person is paid, along with other good management principles, must be individualized: that is, tailored to the person and the situation.

Stimulate your thinking by considering which of the following factors you feel has no relationship to the salary a person receives:

1. The respect he obtains from other employees,
2. His self-confidence,
3. His urge to work hard,
4. His loyalty to the company,
5. His sense of security,
6. His response to your leadership,
7. His shopping around for a new job.

Each of these involves a basic urge and, if overlooked, will hinder your ability to manage to get what you want.

You'll find yourself in a much better position to discuss this subject if you set up regular periods for going over an employee's objectives and his progress toward accomplishing these work targets.

Any differences must be talked out. As a manager, don't ever fall back to a defensive position. You must take the attitude that:

1. A subordinate has a right to discuss his wage rates with you.
2. A subordinate is honest and wants only what he thinks he is entitled to receive.
3. Wage rates are a barometer of the individual's work value to your department, section, or unit.
4. An employee should be paid as much as is practical. Then you can expect outstanding performance.
5. The two of you must fully understand each other.

It's up to you to make sure that what is expected is clearly established. Hopefully, this can be done with the subordinate's concurrence; and, better yet, give him an opportunity to set his own goals. You may use whatever method seems best to you in reaching this accord, but be sure there is a meeting of the minds as to what will be done.

Guiding Practices in Handling
Difficult At-Work Problems

You also need to be aware that the other person's general state of mind has a bearing on how well he is able to do the assigned job.

Sidney Sayer was one of the best electric welders on the pre-fabrication production line. Tom Grover, the supervisor, could always depend on Sid to be at his place at the start of the shift and to do a quality job throughout the day.

The welder was the leader of his crew. Tom summed up Sid's influence as stemming from:

1. Limitless optimism,
2. Knowledge of what to do no matter how difficult the problems,
3. Willingness to help out when someone needed a lift,
4. Fast and perfect workmanship which added to the crew's pool earnings.

One day Sid turned sour. He had nothing to say to his friends and was deeply engrossed in his own thoughts. His welding operation was carried out mechanically. In fact, several prefab sections went by on the line without Sid bothering to even look them over, much less finish the seams. Tom asked his star welder what was troubling him, but Sid only snapped an unpleasant, "Nothing."

By listening to the comments of the other employees, Tom learned that Sid's wife had left him for another man. This destroyed a marriage of ten years; and the welder's two sons, eight and six years of age, were without a mother to help with their care and development.

The supervisor talked with Sid, using the approach that he had heard the welder was having some home troubles and suggesting that a few days off might be of help in getting his problems straightened out. The employee was hostile. Sid said he was all right and needed to keep busy to get his mind off his troubles. The supervisor then firmly told Sid that faulty production was wrecking their past excellent record, the wages of other workmen were suffering, and he must insist that Sid either meet the job requirements or take some time off. The welder became angry, pulled off his protective equipment, threw it on the floor, and walked off the job.

If you were in Tom's place, what would you do?

Fortunately, Tom Grover knew the manager of the local State Employment Office which was the contact for all people seeking work. He called this official and told him Sid's story. His friend agreed to urge the headstrong employee to come back to see Tom. After a few days, Sid came out to the factory; and, following a heart-to-heart talk, Tom gave him a less important spot on the production line, with assurance that proper behavior would earn him his former key position.

You can't entirely avoid similar problems, but to build a better base as an effective manager:

1. Be approachable.

2. In replying when asked for advice about doctors, religion, or investments, always make it clear that your answers are personal opinions—which you should qualify and/or support with objective facts.

3. Show interest in your associates' good health. Urge them to guard this valuable asset. You can provide an example, but don't sell them your health program as necessarily good for their physical well-being.

4. Practice exemplary conduct in the way you talk, act, and live. This expresses your philosophy. Do not try to convert others.

5. Avoid specific investment recommendations unless you can be sure that the recipient fully understands all the risks.

In general, your associations on the job will be more pleasant if both you and the people with whom you work understand that *at-work* friendships and *away-from-work* friendships are different spheres. Each should be cultivated on its own, independent of the other.

Closely related to these "wants" are some widely held beliefs valuable to you as a manager.

How to Use Personal Rights for Better Results

"Eighty per cent of Bell and Howell's sales are from products that were not in existence seven years ago. General Dynamics reports 95 per cent of its sales did not exist in their present form—in some cases, any form—a decade ago. Corning Glass gets 75 per cent of its income from products developed since 1940.

"Creativity has generated this kind of change and its benefits to business are obvious.

"Many companies have a policy of freedom and a fat budget in corporate research, since some managers believe it may be the sole answer to managing creative people. . . .

"They believe management restricts creative thought processes needed to arrive at new conclusions. The creative person—they say— is a very special type whose mind needs freedom to range unharnessed over new areas of scientific inquiry. . . .

"And such an approach leads to the dilemma Westinghouse management recently found itself in when it examined the progress and accomplishments of a well-funded, 'creative' scientist at its Research Laboratories—and found nothing. There is a happy ending to this story, however, because a lot of new ideas and new thinking were going on at Westinghouse at that time. A new management organization was giving the company a streamlined look that in 1965 helped us break records on just about everything—net income, sales billed, new orders, and backlog of unfilled orders.

"This kind of new thinking also reached into our Research Laboratories and the scientist—so used to license—was thrust into a new working environment, which offered him merely freedom. He was asked to agree to clear-cut objectives, which he helped in large part to select, a budget, and to a reasonable schedule of periodic goals with sensible reporting periods. . . .

". . . we can testify to the results. They were excellent. The accomplishments were valuable to the company and satisfying to the scientist." [2]

Marshall K. Evans' comments point out a difficult directional problem for all managers and also suggests an answer.

You must continually remind yourself that most of the people reporting to you have a strong belief in their personal rights: nobody is going to shove them around.

Since the people who feel strongest about their personal rights may be employees who can help you the most, it's good business to work at getting the best results from them. To apply effective management techniques, you must:

1. Figure out and use something which creative persons consider a personal gain.

2. Provide leadership and guidance. Don't let them run wild.

3. Avoid the use of force as much as possible.

4. Provide as much challenge to their initiative as possible.

5. Extend this kind of personal-rights treatment to all your subordinates because creative people don't wear a special badge, and they might be where you least expect to find them.

Strengthen Your Management Base by Helping People Do What They Want to Do

Closely related to personal rights is a person's desire to choose his own way of making a living. Management can't permit everyone to do just as he pleases since there must be organization. You must have defined work areas, and a concerted effort toward predetermined goals. However, you can reach these targets—more quickly, with less cost, and reduced friction—if you can give employees jobs they want to do. People perform best when they enjoy their work.

Sam Smyth was the superintendent of a large factory assembly operation. Four levels of managers, directing a total of approximately 3,000 workmen, reported to Sam. This was a hectic, pressure-packed, everyday strain which can make even some of the best managers fly apart. However, the superintendent had grown up in this environment where original problems continually popped up and quick decisions were necessary. He loved it.

Jay Gardner, the vice-president in charge of manufacturing, came

by Sam's office one day and gave him a big pitch about how badly
the company needed him to plan a completely new manufacturing
layout. Sam agreed to give the assignment a try, and three men
were placed under his direction. At first, the former superintendent
bounced into the office in the morning, sending his three subordinates bustling to pick up a blueprint, look over some equipment,
and study some materials in process. Then he would sit back to
think. But everything was too quiet: he missed the tensions and excitement which result when lots of people strive to do a difficult job
together as a team.

As time went by Sam showed progressively less zip. He agreed
with his subordinates' suggestions without questioning them. Finally
he went to Jay with the request that he go back to his old job. The
manufacturing vice-president briefly explored what had been accomplished before he reversed his original decision and started the dis-
ruptive procedure of returning Sam to the assembly department.
This meant that a place had to be found for Sam's successor and,
eventually, several new people who had been brought into that shop.
And Jay still had to find someone competent to handle the important layout planning job.

You:

1. Can't get the best from people until you are sure of their strengths
   and desires.

2. Shouldn't make a major organization change without a knowledge
   of the special interests of those affected.

3. Will find guides for decision making in past experience and current
   performance.

4. Need to work toward determining what your subordinates view
   as worthwhile work.

5. Must keep assignments, as nearly as possible, in the employee's
   general area of interest.

When you can get people really involved in their jobs they'll accept responsibility for their actions, and then you're managing to
get what you want.

How to Acknowledge the Importance of Others
to Build Your Base as a Manager

Chester Barstow was a department manager for Sunshine Limited, Inc., a small plastics manufacturing plant. One of the longtime employees, Simon Cerylon, was a skilled operator of Sunshine's most important tubing machine. The workman had little formal education but was a shrewd observer of human nature. Through study and experience, Simon had acquired the know-how to influence his fellow employees.

The plastic plant workers' union at Sunshine Limited, Inc., also represented the local public transportation company employees. The 50 bus company workmen had been wrangling and quarreling with management for several months without reaching an agreement. It appeared that a breakoff of negotiations with the bus company would result in a strike which could cause a sympathy walkout of the 300 Sunshine plastic plant workmen.

Mr. Barstow had conscientiously worked to establish a bond of confidence between himself and his subordinates. The manager knew that Simon was buying a small farm, putting two children through college, liked his work, and enjoyed the respect he had earned from the other employees.

Thus, when the tube machine operator asked for some information on the bus company dispute, Barstow directed him to the right place to get these facts:

1. The transportation company employees had comparable wage rates with Sunshine.
2. The bus company furnished lunches free because of schedule requirements. Hospital benefits and also pensions were equal to those received by employees of the plastic company.
3. The demands of the bus company employees were so unreasonable that, if granted, the transit company would have to go out of business.

After talking with some of his fellow workmen, Simon attended the union meeting and made such a strong case for what he believed that he was appointed to the negotiating committee. This group was able to pare down the demands, propose an equitable settlement of all the differences, and get it without a strike.

Chester Barstow set a pattern you might apply, with advantage, to your specific management job. He:

1. Built a good, solid relationship base with employees over a long period of time.
2. Knew what he could do without violating labor laws.
3. Acted with confidence and courage.
4. Permitted Simon to proceed on his own judgment.
5. Subordinated his own role and allowed the tube machine operator to take the leadership.

SUMMARY

1. Keep driving yourself.
2. Learn how to use self-interest.
3. Meet the normal desires of others by:
    (a) Helping subordinates do a better job.
    (b) Meeting their output needs.
    (c) Encouraging efficiency.
    (d) Furthering the family-pride urge.
    (e) Making wages fully equitable.
    (f) Using tested *at-work* practices.
4. Make use of others' convictions by:
    (a) Supporting personal rights.
    (b) Helping them do what they want to do.
    (c) Acknowledging their importance.

NOTES TO CHAPTER 1

[1] Robert Dubin, *Human Relations in Administration*, 2nd ed. (Englewood Cliffs, N. J.: Prentice-Hall, Inc., © 1961), p. 51.

[2] Marshall K. Evans, "A Corner on the Creativity Market," *Advanced Management Journal*, Vol. 32, No. 1 (January, 1967), pp. 36-37.

2

How to Handle
Your Resources

One of the foundation stones in your base as a successful manager is to adequately meet the unlimited desires of your subordinates, superiors, customers, and suppliers with the limited resources at your disposal. You'll find it helpful to remember Edmund Burke's statement: "Every human benefit and enjoyment, every virtue and every prudent act,—is founded on compromise and barter."

As you build your management success base, you'll profit by maintaining a relaxed attitude which will enable you to adjust conflicting or opposing claims, positions, or feelings by reciprocal modifications of demands or mutual concessions.

Will Carson, the department manager of a St. Louis, Missouri, sheet metal fabrication shop, had a problem common to all manufacturers operating 24 hours a day: a majority of employees dislike to work the night shifts. Here are cases involving two night-shift employees. Ted Soer (the hydraulic press operator) served on the town council of suburban Fairfield and was also chief of the volunteer fire department. One day Will received a call from an attorney acquaintance who was a resident of Fairfield and legal adviser to the town council. The lawyer explained how badly Ted was needed for his fire-protection duties and for the council's evening meetings to help solve zoning problems resulting from a building boom in progress in their little village.

The department manager tried to explain that he was sympathetic, but granting such a request could disrupt working relationships. However, Will agreed to check the possibilities. A few days later, a local preacher called Will to plead the necessity for Hugh Kirkman, a skilled electrical maintenance workman, to attend evening meetings of the finance committee, the commission on missions, and the official board (of which he was chairman). These activities required Hugh's presence at least two nights a week in addition to Sundays.

This list could be extended with unlimited, similar illustrations. However, these two should be sufficient to make the point that, usually, the good people who intercede for employees such as Ted and Hugh have no conception of Will's problems in trying to meet their requests. The lawyer and minister, being human, naturally are concerned first and foremost with what they personally want to accomplish.

How to Build Public Relations

You, your associates, and all employees are helped and/or hindered by your heritage, culture, environment, and experience. So, as you attempt to reconcile your desires and those of others with your own convictions, you often find them bumping into one another. For instance, Will's first responsibility is to run an efficient department. This requires that the hydraulic press operate on each shift and that the electrical equipment function continuously.

A second factor to consider is that, in Will's department, it has been a long-established custom that employees work shifts in accordance with their seniority; that is, the longest continuous company service—first, or the day shift; second, late afternoon and evening; third, early mornings. In the past, several exceptions had been made in instances where two employees with the same job voluntarily traded shifts for their own benefit. Such exchange was not encouraged. It always caused discontent and growling among employees who disliked their assigned shift, and it drew comments from them that they would willingly learn a new job to get off the second or third shift.

So, while the department manager wanted to be helpful, it seems evident that the attorney and the pastor did not know how the granting of their requests might well disrupt a smoothly running department. This spotlights a first problem for Will, and one you might come up against as well. Peter F. Drucker sums it up in these words: "But the first social responsibility of the manager today is to make understandable to the laymen—the educated people who are outside of business and necessarily ignorant of it—what it is that business does, can do and should do, and what it is the manager is doing." [1]

Will must try to make these facts clear to the lawyer and the preacher, along with just how Ted and Hugh are involved in the important work which he is trying to accomplish.

The second action which the department manager must take is to consider what he might do to assist these two employees and their interested professional friends without upsetting his department. To do this: (1) Will had to find out what Ted and Hugh thought of the suggested change of shift. (2) When each workman agreed to the change, the department manager next investigated possible effects upon production. (This is really a key assessment because any handicap to productivity will kill the change.) (3) When all checks proved favorable, then Will told Ted and Hugh that it was up to them to find their counterparts on the other shifts who were willing to change. (4) When this was done, each workman signed a statement of understanding about all the details of the change with the effective time spelled out.

This succession of actions took a lot of Will's time but is a way to handle a difficult problem which involves your responsibility for efficient production, the need to maintain good employee relationships, and the necessity of building public goodwill.

How to Earn Growth

Another way to gain public acceptance is to expand your quality products and services to more people. The bite of the "want-more" bug keeps saying, "You can't stand still, either as a manager or as a company." You must either move forward or fall back. Change is coming whether you are ready for it or not. Basic to the foundation of your career is:

1. Getting complete values from your present products and methods.
2. Preparing for the full exploitation of your future opportunities.

Howard Miflin, the general sales manager for a nationally known household appliance manufacturer, at a recent top management staff meeting, enumerated distributors' complaints about their garbage disposals. He listed frequent service calls which uncovered faulty assemblies, excess noise when operating, short-circuited systems, and stalled cutters.

The plant manager, Walter Brazor, asked the chief inspector what the trouble was. This manager blamed it on the tight labor market which had forced them to use inexperienced employees, resulting in some substandard units being released.

Walter then wanted to know what was being done to remedy the difficulty. He was told that an intensive training program for workmen had started with: (1) expertly planned and conducted sessions, (2) attention directed to the known errors and emphasis on speedy corrections, (3) a proven teach-and-check formula in use to make sure right methods were being learned, (4) practical application of skills by putting the employees to work on the production line,

(5) stiffer inspection standards and a more thorough examination of final products.

Brazor told the chief inspector and manufacturing superintendent that this sounded like a proper solution. He then wanted to know from the research specialist, Sylvester Harms, what he was doing to give them a product with broader appeal.

Sylvester called a subordinate to bring in a working model of a disposal which: (1) he held in one hand; (2) when turned on, operated the cutter blades at terrific speed, but no sound could be heard; (3) would fit in a normal-sized drainpipe without special installation; and (4) had a miniature, rubber-mounted motor which would outlast two sets of tungsten steel blades.

Walter Brazor pointed out two principles which you as an effective manager need to remember. Keep:

1. Thinking and working to meet the current market demands.
2. Looking to the future with a product which offers a special appeal to both old and new customers.

This company now has few complaints from distributors and is steadily increasing its share of the market. Such results require thought and an understanding of some of the difficulties you face.

Meet the "Nobody-Likes-to-Be-Wrong" Handicap

Peter Drucker calls a manager's commitment to a fixed position "investments in managerial ego." Mr. Drucker enlarges upon this thought by explaining that: "This is the product that should be a success—but is not. But management has invested so much in the product by way of pride and skill that it refuses to face reality. The product, management is convinced, will succeed tomorrow—but tomorrow never comes.

"... Ford's Edsel venture ... (was) the most publicized American product fiasco. Actually the Edsel was the kind of failure that cannot, as a rule, be foreseen and prevented. What made it a big failure was simply that Ford is a very big company and the automobile market a very big market. And Ford dropped the Edsel fast and recovered rapidly without lasting ill-effects.

"But few people outside the automobile industry realize that another automobile company was nearly destroyed by clinging for almost a quarter-century to an investment in managerial ego. . . . It was a near-failure rather than a total one. For a quarter-century every survey showed that the car was the best engineered car, that it was styled and priced for the largest share of the market, and that the American public loved it.

"The only thing wrong was that the American public did not buy it. . . .

"When, after 25 years, the car was finally dropped, it had all but sucked dry what had been a powerful, successful, and growing company." [2]

So, as a part of the solid foundation for your career as a successful manager, keep in mind that you can best avoid being wrong by developing right relationships with your subordinates. It'll help to remember and use these "don'ts":

1. Be hard-nosed about any personal position after it becomes clear that you are wrong.
2. Make an issue out of isolated mistakes of subordinates.
3. Forget that success on your job depends upon correct information from subordinates.
4. Fail to let those reporting to you know that you depend upon their reliability.
5. Let your concern for hurting another's feelings prevent an understanding by subordinates of the dangers of misleading information.

In times past, the production manager was the only "boss" in a manufacturing department. Today, however, there are usually several levels of supervision plus service and associate managers with specific responsibilities. Each of these people can take independent action; thus the production shop manager is in a delicate coordinating position as he walks the relationship tightrope to obtain efficient output.

For instance, foreman Ed Stigler, in an Ohio housewares plant, was in charge of a production line turning out enameled teakettles. About the middle of the morning shift, Ed was excitedly informed by Terry Roop, the chief inspector, that his teakettles were showing a sizable crack running diagonally across the rounded surface. Over-hearing this conversation, Jack Helford, the scheduling supervisor, warned Ed that a line shutdown at that time—because of idle time payments, committed deliveries, and inventory storage costs—would cost more than scrapping a few teakettles. Bob James, the manager in charge of maintenance, seemed to second the no-stoppage idea. He told Ed that his orders were to grease-pack all the conveyor bearings on the next line shutdown, and such a job required 12 hours.

Ed looked at the distinctive crack which was causing the in-spectors to reject about one out of four of the finished teakettles. Then he went back along the production line, carefully watching each operation: painting, priming, shaping, trimming. In the form-ing operation, four punch presses used identical dies to round off the semifinished steel, and the output from these four machines was combined on a belt conveyor to be taken to the next step, a shearing operation. As a manager who knew his machines, Ed felt sure that the trouble must come from the punch press forming operation. Terry and Bob, after seeing Ed carefully examine the work coming from each of the presses, volunteered that they had already thought of this possibility but had found the pieces O.K. Each speculated that it had to be something more serious than a bad forming die.

Even though the materials looked all right, the production man-ager reasoned that the presses must be the trouble spot. He had each operator stamp out a piece which he carried to the shears. After being cut, the material from number two press showed the hairline crack, while the steel from the other presses came out O.K. Just to be sure, Ed repeated the test—with the same results.

The production manager shut down the number two press until Bob could arrange to have the necessary repairs made to the faulty die. This enabled the remainder of the shop to continue operating.

Ed Stigler's teakettle trouble-spotting suggests several foundation stones you can use as a base to help you develop as a manager and do your part to satisfy the bite of the "want-more" bug:

1. Recognize your important problems and tackle them.
2. Don't let others' conversation prevent your using your best judg-ment.

3. Recognize the broad impact your decisions can have in solving a complex industrial problem.

4. Keep in mind that you need good information to be a successful manager.

5. There is nothing like competently handling a difficult production problem to strengthen your leadership with both your associates and the employees reporting to you.

So, while you need to appreciate that nobody likes to be wrong, as a manager you must be ready to step up to your job responsibility and make corrections when things go wrong.

Benefit from the "What-Have-You-Done-for-Me-Lately?" Attitude

A basic problem-solving principle which should be instilled in those people reporting to you is a willingness to follow your directions. Such a goal is best accomplished when the subordinate can see some gain for himself in doing what you want done.

This opens one of the particular challenges of your job because you are continually required to revitalize your follower's belief in you as his leader. Thus, while the phrase "What have you done for me lately?" may seem like a cynicism, it is nevertheless a fact in your everyday life as a manager.

A large manufacturer and distributor of TV sets in Indiana used superior wiring as a quality asset in its product advertising. To maintain this good workmanship and efficient output, Department 327 was established to solder connections, identify, group, and test the hundreds of wires going into the company's TV sets. In this key operation, both careful workmanship and close control of costs were vital to the success of the company. The employees were paid on a pool piecework basis.

The management organization of Department 327 consisted of three levels: a department manager, Sam Esty; a group chief supervisor, Joe Steen, with two supervisors who each directed 20 employees (principally women) as they carried out the assembly operation. Also reporting to the department manager was Clem Muse, chief supervisor of procurement, who purchased, stored, and delivered the wire to the assemblers. Clem had under his direction two supervisors responsible for the performance of several buyers as well as traffic and warehousing specialists.

In studying the weekly wire scrap report, the department manager noticed that it showed a 100 per cent increase over the previous week. Sam also recalled having read in a trade magazine that an industry-wide steel strike was expected to start early in the next month. So the manager of Department 327 promptly set up a session with his key subordinates.

In this meeting Joe Steen explained that his two supervisors were feuding over who should train the newly hired employees; and, in his efforts to settle the quarrel, he had overlooked the rise in scrap rate. It also came to light in the meeting that one of Clem Muse's supervisors had covered up for an employee. This buyer had approved and sent to the production area a sizable shipment of wire from their single supply source—wire which had not been quality-checked in accordance with specifications. This gave Joe an out, and he promptly declared that it was no wonder his scrap had increased.

Check the answer indicating your opinion of how these managers might have improved their performance:

		Yes	No
Sam Esty:			
1.	Should let others worry about scrap reports or steel strikes.	___	___
2.	Should have spent more time building relationships with subordinates.	___	___
3.	Should not have called a meeting.	___	___
4.	Should have known Joe's and Clem's weaknesses.	___	___
Joe Steen:			
5.	Should have fired his feuding supervisors.	___	___
6.	Should have established a standard practice for training newly hired employees.	___	___
7.	Should have required more businesslike discipline.	___	___

Joe Steen (Cont.)

8. Should have changed the method of payment to straight hourly rate.   ____ ____

9. Should have set up a control to warn him of out-of-line increases in scrap.   ____ ____

10. Should have used self-control and not tried to alibi the increased scrap.   ____ ____

Clem Muse: *Yes*   *No*

11. Should have defended the supervisor who failed to correct his buyer's mistake.   ____ ____

12. Should have made preparation to fill production needs if the steel strike did occur.   ____ ____

13. Should have arranged for a tighter quality-control check of materials.   ____ ____

14 Should have arranged for alternate sources of wire supply.   ____ ____

The correct answers are: (1) no (2) yes (3) no (4) yes (5) no (6) yes (7) yes (8) no (9) yes (10) yes (11) no (12) yes (13) yes (14) yes.

Excellent managers should score: 12 right.
Good managers should score: ten right.
Anything less: Study your job more thoroughly.

Steen was soon transferred to another shop. Clem Muse was warned and given 60 days in which to make drastic improvements in his management controls. Several of the lower-level managers in both shops were reduced or transferred.

The lessons of Department 327 show you the best way you can answer an employee's question, "What have you done for me lately?" Be sure you apply effective management techniques the very best way you know how all day, every day, and keep learning to continuously improve your job performance.

Remember, the principal ingredient in good management is *you,* and you should make the most of the opportunities offered by your job responsibilities to get friction-free cooperation.

Watch for These Desires

Even if you had the touch of King Midas and a gadget with the powers of Aladdin's lamp, employees would find something further to desire outside your magic powers to supply. People are endowed with an insatiable want for greater rewards and benefits: more money, more security, more automobiles, more houses, more prestige, more power, and other evidences of tangible wealth.

Also, you can't afford to overlook the intangible urges. The bite of the "want-more" bug is equally important to you as a manager whether it is evident as a desire for physical goods or an untouchable want. To meet these intangible wants, you must gear your effort toward supplying those reporting to you with:

1. Satisfaction from their work, a feeling that they are going someplace; a job they like; an opportunity to put something special into their work to prepare themselves for a better future goal.

2. Help in keeping up with the "Joneses," in having the respect of people important to them, in being accepted as equals by their neighbors. Remember that people are social beings, seeking the approval of others.

3. A chance to cultivate self-reliance and a working atmosphere which typifies the personal kinds of "want-more" urges, such as go-ahead self-discipline. This desirable goal is a fragile quality nourished by stimulating initiative, commending performance, and guarding the individual's right to be different.

How to Use a Little to Accomplish a Lot

As you work toward establishing a solid base for your standing room to forge ahead to success in management, you frequently find your ammunition limited. Thus you must make good use of what you have available.

During the American Civil War, from a total U. S. population of only 32 million in all of the states, the men actively engaged in fighting by the opposing armies reached 4 million. Even though the

Confederacy, before the war was over, conscripted all males 14 to 60 years of age, their combat force did not at any time equal one-half the number of soldiers in the Northern Army. Yet the South waged an extremely costly war for over three years in which they barely missed winning on several occasions.

However, the weight of numbers and economic collapse—the Northern States had 66 percent of the railroad mileage, 81 percent of the factories, and 75 percent of the wealth [3]—proved too much for even the master Confederate strategist, General Lee. General Grant's superiority in numbers of soldiers isn't clear, but he speaks of 115,000 reinforced by 40,000; and when Lee was forced to surrender at Appomattox on April 9, 1865, his starving and completely exhausted army was estimated at 26,000 to 28,000. A good example of using a little to accomplish a great deal.

You can earn the respect of others as a manager by your performance and accomplish a great deal through judicious use of scarce resources. Suppose you have seven employees reporting to you and your finance department allots you a merit raise fund of $500 in the first half of the year. In this situation you may take several courses: (1) Divide the available money equally. (2) Make the awards in graduated amounts according to time spent on the payroll. (3) Use the funds to recognize outstanding performance.

The first two listed alternatives do not require any management know-how, judgment, or courage. The third is the method you must use to "make a little accomplish a lot." It's this kind of can-do management which earns the respect of your colleagues. By such actions your associate managers and those reporting to you observe and admire your capabilities.

Remember that quality performance is always in short supply.

Basically there is little difference in the manager who succeeds and the one who fails in his assignment, but what little there is carries a lot of weight. You must more effectively use:

1. Scarce superior skills.
2. Development efforts to add valuable talents.
3. Refine and conserve natural resources.

4. Creative imagination to uncover productive innovations.

5. Liquid capital judiciously.

6. Self-restraint and personal discipline.

Deferred personal satisfaction and wise choices will enable you to stretch these short-supply items into high-return performance.

How to Pick Payoff Values

As a leader of others, charged with the requirement to get your results through their efforts, you'll find that on-the-target rifle shots are more effective than shotgun blasts. You'll be safe in accepting the fact that people want their jobs to:

1. Provide them with meaningful work.

2. Get them more material things.

3. Build safeguards against future loss of income.

4. Supply them a chance for growth as individuals.

5. Help them look well to others.

6. Allow them to have a part in saying what happens to them.

7. Have their leader give them some personal attention.

Recognizing all these desires, it is up to you to determine how each of these universal wants will be met and how you can apply them in your particular management job.

Ray Stoff, a manager in industrial engineering for a large metal-working plant on the West Coast, explored the methods by which a good manager might be recognized for using the magic seven rifle shots. Basically, Ray wanted to establish a procedure by which the general manager would be notified of exceptional performance by lower-level managers. The boss would then commend the most deserving by one or both ways: a letter and/or personally in a meeting. A practical difficulty in Ray's plan was getting the information for the general manager without upsetting the organization. For instance, it was bad to have: (1) managers feel they were being spied on, (2) faulty practices of managers handled unwisely, and (3) too many routine matters cluttering up the boss' demanding time schedule.

Stoff considered the idea of a staff man with this assigned responsibility, but finding the right man would be difficult because he must be: (1) a competent manager, (2) one who had earned the confidence of other managers, (3) knowledgeable about company operations, and (4) able to evaluate superior management actions in complex relationships.

After assessing the dangers and handicaps of the staff-man approach, Ray Stoff decided to suggest the idea to his division manager. The engineer recommended that the regular line management should identify those individuals deserving special commendation. Since the boss accepted Ray's idea, test yourself by marking the principles "good" or "bad" which you consider proper in proposing, adopting, or implementing a new idea or method:

		Good	*Bad*
1.	You must never rock the boat.	____	____
2.	Can I use it to make a rival manager look incompetent?	____	____
3.	The end results I hope to achieve.	____	____
4.	A flood of ideas always pays off for the suggester.	____	____
5.	Watch for dangers and pitfalls which might hamper the changed method.	____	____
6.	What must be done to reach your objective?	____	____
7.	There is only one way to accomplish what I want to do.	____	____
8.	I'll welcome others' help in figuring out how to make the idea work.	____	____
9.	Give others as much credit as you honestly can.	____	____

Answers: (1) bad (2) bad (3) good (4) bad (5) good (6) good (7) bad (8) good (9) good.

If you properly identified seven or more principles, you're good at picking the payoff values.

How You Can Benefit from Some Significant Techniques

To satisfy the bite of the "want-more" bug and build your success base, you need to know some of the significant features of effective management techniques. To make any enterprise possible, several of these features must be in operation, such as:

1. Total production must consistently leave something in the bank for investments in capital goods. You can't pay out all your earnings as expenses or dividends because it's up to you to remain competitive in an advancing technology. You must keep an eye on the efficiency of your equipment, tools, and plant to insure that reinvestment equals or exceeds depreciation.

2. There is a division of effort—specialization.This means that each individual qualifies himself as an expert by repeating the same activity or operation. Yours is a threefold responsibility in this area: to determine capabilities, to make proper assignments, and to encourage the development of each person's strongest potential.

3. The customer must be satisfied. You must deliver quality of service and/or product. Whatever your place in your organization, the pressure is on you to see that a standard is met. The people reporting to you pace themselves by what they see you do, so just good enough to get by will not get the results you need.

4. It is easy for people to go where they wish to sell their services or buy their products. This mobility means that you have a persuading job to do. As a practical influencer, directing the work of others, you'll find that frequently it is necessary to compromise and accept something less than the performance you would like to have. Often you must arrange your work so that you get the best results with available skills while you plan and build toward future improvements. Such a test keeps you alert and thinking for more efficient operations.

5. The value of money should be relatively stable. While prices have increased, wage levels have also risen. In a money exchange

economy, your headaches are increased if price levels gyrate wildly. Constructive planning for material, wages, and sales costs presents another unpredictable variable. When a careful estimate can put this problem to bed, you can direct more attention to other problems.

6. The market determines the reward. In spite of a local situation in which a strong union may be able to force high and unrealistic wage rates, or when extreme need for a special skill might temporarily cause an out-of-balance return to selected individuals, it is generally true that payments for services are the result of demand and supply in a "who-can-do-the-job-best" environment. Likewise, your own advancement in your organization is normally directly determined by your job performance.

Individuals and companies have been assisted by one or more of these listed features, but often their success has been limited because they failed to have all six of these characteristics going for them as you can. These unique features give your management job its peculiar success advantage.

It is important in building a foundation in your profession to determine how to apply all six of these special attributes to your management job.

How to Get Your Share of the Prize Money

Obviously, the aim of any business venture is to show a record of steady growth in sales and profits to its owners and the financial community.

You can contribute your part to the profit picture of the manufacturing section of your company by encouraging cost-saving ideas, boosting product quality, and devising new methods to stimulate added production. In marketing, you may win more customers by attractive packaging, a stronger product line, and greater incentives to your salesmen. Whatever your management position, you should remember that the best way for you to get a larger share of the prize money is for you to do everything you possibly can to grow a bigger melon to split.

As you build a larger profit base for greater success in management, four contributors should benefit in proportion to the value which each adds to the total size of the reward. These are:

1. Risk-taking returns for those who supply the capital to make your commercial venture possible.
2. Physical skills which increase the worth of the product or service.
3. The planning and directional abilities, which includes all levels of management.
4. Rents of money, lands, buildings, tools, and other needed fixed assets.

Just who and how much of the extra piece of profit cake goes to these producers is critical for your success. An upward tilt of the progress curve depends upon maintaining a balance of incentives.

For instance, too low risk-taking wages scare off the chance-taker with money to invest. Too high return to those who supply venture capital handicaps payments to the other essential producing entities. Too high wage rates decrease profits and reduce sales, while low wages discourage the development of skills and tend to reduce purchasing power. Too low incentives to managers attract only employees of mediocre ability, reduce the competitive urge, and cater to less than maximum effort. Too high wages for those who supply directional services add unjustified costs which unbalance the value of this profession as one of the necessary ingredients for efficient production. Too high rents encourage savings but tend to reduce borrowing, which can handicap valuable innovations by siphoning off risk money. Too low rents may fail to attract the funds needed for the purchase of buildings and machines.

As a responsible manager, you are the pilot of a delicately balanced mechanism designed to satisfy a need. A most interesting feature of this machine is that the factors which make it go are all striving to satisfy their personal goals. Because of your leadership situation, you might obtain more than your fair share for a short time; however, in a healthy, growing system, this natural desire must be kept within bounds to help establish a solid foundation for your future success as a manager.

SUMMARY

1. Be informed of problems. Analyze and solve them.

2. Be ready:

   (a) To build public relations.

   (b) To get full value from products and services.

3. Recognize that nobody likes to be wrong:

   (a) Get rid of your losers.

   (b) Be tolerant of isolated mistakes.

   (c) Insist upon getting correct information.

   (d) Depend on subordinates.

4. Know your job and act confidently.

5. Recognize employees' desires.

6. Stretch your resources.

7. Pick the payoff values:

   (a) Look at the end results.

   (b) Beware of the dangers.

   (c) Get the big picture.

   (d) Check the alternatives.

   (e) Give credit where it's due.

8. Use these essentials:

   (a) Save something for future investment.

   (b) Make experts of your subordinates.

   (c) Meet customer demands.

   (d) Be flexible in getting the best from employees.

9. Balance needs and goals.

Notes to Chapter 2

[1] Peter F. Drucker, *Managing for Results* (New York: Harper & Row, 1964), pp. 226-27.

[2] Drucker, *Managing for Results*, pp. 60-61.

[3] Clark C. Spence, *The Sinews of American Capitalism* (New York: Hill & Wang, Inc., 1964), p. 147.

3

How to Use a
Secret Weapon

It's always best to get there first with the most. If you learn to use effective management techniques you'll go out in front of your competition, external or internal, and move up to a more responsible management job. Your secret weapon is training and education. To use it, you've got to learn:

How to Operate in the New, Trained-Brain Climate

"A complex society is dependent every hour of every day upon the capacity of its people to read and write, to make complex judgments and to act in the light of fairly extensive information. When there is not this kind of base on which to build, modern social and economic developments are simply impossible." [1]

This advice is not news to most employees in modern business. On your job you continually get questions on: "What can I do to improve my position, my pay, my understanding of what I need to do to get ahead?" This dissatisfaction with the present is a reflection of the individual's appreciation of the rapid pace of new developments.

With such seemingly universal understanding of the need to change with the times—since you are primarily a motivator of others—the presumption might be suggested that you have it made. However, a manager's job is not that simple; in fact, if you are not careful, an avowed desire for improvement can make your job tougher.

Regardless of how hard you strive to find an easy way to gain an educational advantage, personal effort is still required. Schemes, maneuvers, and beating another person to the punch will not help you build the base for your career which you must have. Dishonest techniques under the day-to-day pressure of the job fade away or lose you the confidence you must have to go ahead in your profession.

Since these things are true, how do you fulfill your lifter-upper role in management? Here are some major rules:

First, you must be a leader who really knows the people under your direction. When a valued subordinate says that he wants to improve himself, does he really mean it or is he just fishing for approval? In most instances you should know the answer to this question; if not, you must test. What does he want to do better? Is he thinking of his job? What has he done up to now in this direction?

Second, work to establish that he really does want to make a change. In a discouraging number of cases, you'll find that your subordinate is well satisfied with how he is doing. So you just can't wait until it dawns upon an employee that he really should work a little harder, a little better, and a little longer if he and you are to step up the better-performance ladder.

Third, in directing better educated employees, endeavor to arrange special assignments which will permit the subordinate to recognize his shortcomings for himself. For instance, if you are trying to bring along a younger manager who has an excess of personal ego which causes him to look down on the workmen, arrange to have him supervise some technicians in an area which makes it essential to depend on the regular employees to get the work accomplished.

Fourth, get someone else to make it clear to the employee where he should seek improvement. This must not be taken to mean that it is permissive to let others solve your problems; rather, recognize the fact that at times others not as close to the individual as you are can often "get more house" than you are able to obtain. Doctors, lawyers, teachers, and preachers often exert a special influence that close friends can't. Training directors and educators can gain special attention from an employee which his immediate line supervisor cannot. You should make full use of the detached third party when it'll help you operate better in the newer, more educated employee environment.

Fifth, you should use the urge which most people have to follow a leader who will make them become what they are capable of achieving. This desire increases in strength as knowledge is acquired and ambitions whetted. For instance, if a subordinate is neglecting the improvement of those under his direction, try suggesting that it will be impossible to promote him until he has an understudy ready to take over his job.

Each of these proven rules for the better management of superior and more widely informed employees must be applied with judgment and reinforced by some detailed knowledge of the people reporting to you. This means that you must have an accumulation of data and facts; however, in building a solid base as an effective manager, you can't allow yourself to be overburdened by surplus and unneeded trivia.

How to Avoid the Information Overkill

A flood of meaningless words can make lots of trouble by causing misunderstandings and wasting your limited time.

The boss asked for a status report on the subassembly operation. His subordinate, Hi Jorgan, replied that there was a complaint that tooling had failed to deliver the jigs and fixtures promised the week before. Further, his key setup man had to attend a relative's funeral in Arkansas, and this had posed a manpower problem. Hi went on to explain that purchasing was holding him up on materials; and the intermediate assembly superintendent kept hounding him, making his life miserable about the smallest discrepancy in quality. At this point the questioning superior, exercising self-control, again asked, "But what about your delivery of subassemblies?" Hi said, "Oh, we are meeting our output curve; in fact, we are a few assemblies ahead of schedule. But you have no idea how tough the going is with all our problems. Why, just last week . . ." Here, the boss held up his hand, calling a halt to the deluge of conversation. This exchange is similar to the kind of gobbledygook communication to which you have been or will be exposed in your management experience; and it's one of the things which you can eliminate to get on with the job of creating a more solid foundation for your future. Here are some things you should do for a too vocal subordinate:

1. Stop him quickly when he starts off on a tangent and make it clear that you want a to-the-point report.

2. Direct him to write a biweekly or weekly report of what he wants to tell you.

3. Diplomatically look into his relationships with his associate managers.

4. Don't act hastily, but consider whether you have the wrong manager in a key spot.

Another fast-developing, potential overinformation problem facing the modern manager is caused by the computer. Through this instrument, literally hundreds of thousands of statistics are available for the decision-makers in time for use, a situation which formerly just did not exist. Because it is such a fascinating tool, computers can easily become playthings rather than aids to the manager in helping you to do a better job. Curiosity-inclined managers often try to include every possible variation of the problem they face. This is not only a waste of time and effort, but takes up valuable machine space.

To assist you to build a proper management base through the most effective use of computers, do you agree or disagree with these statements:

		Agree	Disagree
1.	Let each department or section have complete control of the machines they need.	____	____
2.	Acquaint your total management organization with what the machines can do and are doing.	____	____
3.	Hire expert technicians to operate the service.	____	____
4.	Insist upon a careful management review of the requests being made and the expected results from information asked for.	____	____
5.	Establish advanced planning as a regular part of your computer program use.	____	____
6.	Identify scientific and business-type application for clearer understanding for management utilization.	____	____
7.	Disperse the equipment throughout the factory, closest to the using group.	____	____

Your job of discriminating in the use of sophisticated equipment becomes more difficult as improvements are made and more employees become better educated. In the above statements, you should agree with all except number one and number seven. This is part of your education. You must sustain continued personal growth because intelligent support of others is the mark of a successful manager.

Some Benefits You Gain from Better Educated Employees

In a study released in the mid-1960s, it was determined that the higher a person's level of formal education, as a general rule, the greater the individual's earnings, the stronger his belief in self-determination, and the more active he would be in selecting and electing governmental officials. Further, the higher the median level of education in both small and large cities, the greater the volume of retail sales. Even the farmer with the best income will, as a rule, have the better formal education.[2]

When present-day requirements in industry are examined, it is evident that our socioeconomic system could not operate at its current level of output and quality with a majority of workmen whose average schooling was less than that of a high school graduate. Most employees today must be able to correctly figure production percentages. They must be qualified to understand the succession of operations which may reveal leads to excessive scrap or rework of products. With more automation, the bulk of regular workmen are required to correctly read control gauges and be capable of taking the right actions when the recorder gives the wrong answers.

In the office, your greatest helper is a secretary who can spell and type neatly: an assistant with initiative and judgment, with the ability to meet problems when you are not available, in the same general way that you would handle these situations if you were at your desk.

These kinds of employees have assisted the United States—which has approximately 5 percent of the world's population and 6 percent of the land area—to build 40 percent of the world's industrial production. Since no other nation has approached this record, in looking for answers you must seriously consider that the basic reason for this tremendous output is because: (1) 28 percent of our total population was enrolled in school in 1964. Total cash outlays for public and private schools were estimated at $36 billion. Nearly 2¼ million persons were employed as teachers, instructors, and professors.[3] Obviously, education, as one of our greatest industries, did not grow up overnight. It has been years in the making and has helped business develop and prosper as it has expanded. (2) Seemingly, the remainder of the world has overlooked the competitive advantages of education to the extent that it can truly be called our secret weapon. In 1960, in the five-to-19 age group, northern America had 82 percent of these young people enrolled in school. The remainder of the world had an average of 44 percent of their children in this age range in school. The areas most nearly competitive with us were Australia and New Zealand with 68 percent; next, Europe with 62 percent; the lowest area was Africa with 25 percent.[4] (3) A number of recent economic studies have revealed that investment in human capital—education, on-the-job training, health, etc.— has played a much bigger role in the United States' economic growth than previously realized. In *The Sources of Economic Growth in the United States*, Edward F. Denison calculated that the rising educational level of the labor force (including managerial and technical personnel) was responsible for 23 percent of the growth in real national income between 1929 and 1957. Physical capital accounted for only 15 percent, while the general "advance of knowledge" contributed 20 percent. (This latter percentage is undoubtedly a by-product of increased education.)

Economic advancement is not the sole aim of education, since the greatest return to the student will be the fulfillment of his individual capacity for intellectual and personal development. Thus, in the latter Sixties, with more education per person than ever before and investments in plant and equipment also rising rapidly, the world may see an authentic "great leap forward" American style.

With these advantages, the real test you face as a manager is just how effectively you make use of these more highly educated employees who look to you for direction.

How to Use What You Know

Since better education goes hand-in-hand with a greater output, as a successful manager you should:

1. Be guided in your hiring by the prospective employee's total education.

2. Spend as much time as possible helping those people reporting to you to help themselves.

3. Keep up to date on the opportunities available for special-interest education, helpful reading, and self-disciplined study.

To illustrate the advantages gained through applying these principles, let's look at the experience of a Lansing, Michigan, manufacturing firm. Jerry Farnam, a first-level manager in the finance department, approved the hiring of two young fellows named Art and Jim, each in his early twenties with two years of college liberal-arts education. This was the first really serious job for either of the young men. They were assigned clerical work: estimating, checking costs, and posting. It is the practice of this company to make non-college-credit educational classes available to employees at no cost except for their own time spent in attending classes.

Jerry suggested that an accounting class which the education section was just starting would give his newly employed clerks a better feel for their work. Both men enrolled in the hour-and-a-half evening class, held twice a week for eight weeks. Art dug in on the course and found much of the information useful on his job. Jim attended on a hit-and-miss basis, always thinking about some outside attraction of greater interest to him. At the conclusion of the accounting sessions, Jim was relieved to have it over, but Art continued his self-improvement effort by signing up for a business law class. When Jim found out about this extra effort on the part of his fellow employee, he chided him by saying, "Why don't you cut out the grind and have some fun? You're not getting anywhere with that studying. Remember, it is *who* you know, not *what* you know."

Soon the other employees in the office began to find out that Art knew how to solve problems and could answer questions that others fumbled on. More and more they sought his advice. It developed just naturally that Jerry started discussing any important office changes with Art before taking action.

Art is worth more:

I. *To the company* because he:
   1. Produces more on the job.
   2. Will continue to grow and become more valuable.
   3. Is on his way to becoming a successful manager, a real leader.

II. *To the other employees* because he:

  1. Is setting an example for others.

  2. Is adding to the total human resources by encouraging self-discipline.

  3. Is showing others how to approach a solution to their problems.

III. *To himself* because he:

  1. Is refining his personal skills.

  2. Is building himself into a better balanced, more confident personality.

  3. Is adding to his own happiness and self-satisfaction.

  4. Is gaining personal economic security.

When you are able to bring some of your subordinates along so that they perform like Art, then you are building a strong base as an effective manager by making the best use of what you know.

How to Get What You Need More Quickly

In *Through the Looking Glass and What Alice Found There*, the Queen said, "It takes all the running you can do, to keep in the same place. If you want to get somewhere else, you must run at least twice as fast as that!"

Lewis Carroll seems to be saying that there are always greater peaks to scale. As you strive to build a stronger base for your career through the use of your secret weapon, keep reminding yourself that in spite of great achievements you never fully arrive at the ultimate in management performance.

Here's a manager's problem for your study. Ralph Sloan, as superintendent of the fabrication shops in a heating and air conditioner manufacturing plant in the East, was known as a go-getter. The superintendent was always searching for new ways to accomplish his work—perform his operations better. He visited other shops, looking for ideas, and tried new sequences of work flow when time permitted. Unexpectedly faced with a requirement for more base burners than his shop could turn out, Ralph strongly recommended buying a new medium planer. However, the purchasing department found that such equipment could not be delivered for 28 months. The superintendent then proposed that a rebuilt machine could be bought at a local broker's supply house.

The buyers found a planer, but it was priced at $200 more than the cost of a brand-new one. Ralph didn't hesitate in recommending the purchase. He even went out on a limb to explain that the current orders would keep them busy for 18 months, and in that length of time the additional machine would more than pay for itself. At the superintendent's insistence, the planer was obtained. But the machine was a Jonah right from the start. It had an off-standard base which delayed the installation until other shop equipment could be rearranged to make a place for it. And, unfortunately, no one had noticed that the main bearings were worn out and had to be replaced. Ralph also discovered that the gear speed was slower than comparable planers. As he experimented with his nemesis, Ralph removed and replaced gears until he obtained very fast output, but not of the high finished quality needed.

On Monday, after thinking about his problem all weekend, Ralph had all the base burners roughed through the speeded-up planer and final-finished on the other equipment. This required some adjustment in the employees' work habits, so Monday's production was a few parts below normal output. It increased on Tuesday, and by the end of the week, base burners were coming out of the shop in sufficient numbers and quality to meet the stepped-up schedule.

These are some things you can learn from Ralph's experience:

1. He realized the need to keep working for his professional improvement.

2. The superintendent did not let some rather serious mistakes destroy his will to try for a comeback.

3. Ralph showed personal strength and courage.

4. He learned valuable lessons from his mistake.

5. The superintendent didn't hesitate to forge ahead in the face of obstacles to get the experience which every manager must have to build a success foundation.

With judgment, you can add to your win percentage by some calculated chance-taking.

Benefits Through Acting on Your Own Decisions

The ounce of cold sweat which you put out while waiting to see how a planned management move develops builds up more tension than a pound of hot sweat from physical effort. Such pressure situations are one of the hazards of your profession; such risks must be taken if you score as a successful manager.

"Europe today is discovering one of the secrets behind U. S. economic leadership of the world—better businessmen. Americans are getting more out of money, manpower, and materials by managing companies more efficiently, taking more risks. giving better training to executives, and recruiting high-quality young managers." [5]

Which explains something of the climate in which you are often required to call the shots and hope you're right. In a large midwest assembly plant, Garth Crow was a department manager with approximately 300 industrial engineers in his division. Three general supervisors reported to Garth, and two additional levels of managers shared the directional responsibilities of the department.

The department manager had assigned specific responsibilities to his immediate subordinates. These men are designated A—with planning and methods determination and duties; B—the carrying out of time study and efficiency of operations; C—planning for future products and ways to handle such new business. Each of these managers had worked hard to select the right people, train them well, and build a good, solid organization to carry out his responsibilities.

In thinking about how to help his keymen become even better managers, Garth decided a general broadening and greater flexibility would benefit these managers. Thus he decided to shift his top subordinates so that: A was assigned to future products and development, B to planning and methods, and C to time study and efficiency. The purpose of this rotation was carefully explained to each of the affected managers, but C was not happy with his assignment; in fact, he disliked it so much that he resigned and took a job with another company. As might be expected, Garth's boss looked down his nose at this loss of a good man. However, the department manager stood by his decision and raised his best man on the second level to take C's spot, filling in behind him with a good man from the first level. This unexpected resignation caused Garth to spend greater effort in seeing that the new manager adjusted to the more demanding duties; but, in a relatively short time, all units were functioning satisfactorily.

Seven months after manager C accepted his new job with the other company, he suffered a nervous breakdown and was hospitalized for extensive psychiatric treatment. It was reported that he failed to adjust to his new duties.

Let's look at some of the gains Garth made in acting upon his decision:

1. He put into operation some intelligent planning for the future of his important subordinates.

2. The department manager used a meaningful selection device to identify and prove his better follow-up men.

3. The department had the benefit of the best new ideas and operating practices from more than one superior in more than a single section.

4. The top manager determined who could be counted on to cooperate in building a more efficient organization.

5. Garth gained confidence in his own judgment.

6. He demonstrated to his superior that his decisions were not lightly made, but, rather, weighed with consideration of possible obstacles.

7. Garth met a difficult problem in forthright fashion.

These benefits suggest an additional area where you can work to improve your management base.

How to Worry Less and Work More

One day the section manager stopped by the office of his subordinate, Cal Benedict, and announced, "Starting the first of the month, the heat treat shop which you have been managing will be transferred to Serge Grover's supervision." Seeking to soften the blow, the boss quickly added, "But don't you worry. This will give you more time to direct the mat curing process."

Regardless of this assurance, Cal did get plenty concerned. He asked himself questions about what he had been doing wrong, who might have been talking about his methods of managing, what Serge had shown the boss that he hadn't, and how long it might be before some other of his present functions would be given to another manager. It is natural that he would worry: the profession of management gives rewards and credits, but it is also a tough and impersonal taskmaster. You must produce or get out of the way for a more deserving manager. Evidently Cal didn't have "heat treat" very high on his "give-attention" list or he would not have lost this activity. It is most likely true that Serge set as one of his objectives the acquiring of the added responsibility which the boss turned over to him, because such things seldom happen by chance.

Since one of the real powers of our economic-influenced social system is its ability to flex and react to all kinds of pressures, your basic attitude as a manager is more important to your success than your techniques of operation.

Worry—an attitude—stems from a way of looking at your job and is an initiative killer. This is the very thing you need most. So you must dispose of as many sources of concern as practical. Most managers agree that if they can get on top of their jobs they can act with confidence, discard unproductive worries, and meet their ever-changing work requirements. In cultivating such an operating management attitude, you must:

1. Truly accept that you can only succeed through the job performance of others. Thus, you may do the detail work, not to "show up" those who happen to be your subordinates, but rather to set an example or suggest a better way and so encourage those reporting to you toward a more effective output.

2. Avoid the use of your authority as the boss to order a subordinate to do a job. You must have this ultimate power; but the more that the members of your crew or group can be persuaded that it is to their interest to involve themselves for the success of the project, the less you need to be concerned about building your base as a professional manager.

3. Establish a priority of values on your particular job.

These management attitudes can reduce the personal pressures of your tension-acclimated assignment by setting your goal to achieve results through the efforts of others, by saving direct orders for the must-have-immediate-action cases, and by being alert to the parts of your work essential to your success.

As you get on top of your job, you realize that an important part of a manager's job is good communication. This means not only sending orders down but also the free flow of ideas, proposals, and suggestions up the line from the people reporting to you.

How You Can Gain by "Staying Off Your Dignity"

June 18, 1815—if Napoleon had been willing to relax what he considered his infallible military judgment sufficiently to listen to the misgivings of such peninsular veterans as his subordinate generals, Soult, Reille, and Foy, the outcome of the Battle of Waterloo likely would have been different. Instead, France's emperor drew up his 74,000 gallant soldiers in three lines supported by 246 guns in full view, 1300 yards in front of the Anglo-Dutch army. Napoleon was determined to break Wellington's center instead of outflanking his left and separating him from the Prussian General Blücher's support. The French emperor's temperament was such that his subordinates hesitated to suggest valuable ideas, even though they were familiar with some of the Iron Duke's tactics and appreciated the dangers to the French army if even a minor hitch in the battle plan developed. Several unexpected events did occur, such as French marshals Ney and Gronchy misreading their orders, plus Wellington and Blücher's unexpectedly strong determination to join forces.

As an effective manager you must never fail to make full use of your subordinates' knowledge and experience. To do this, you can't stand on your position of authority, aloof from the people whose full support you must have to succeed on the job. An exceptional leader thinks first about how he can get better support from those under his direction.

Some Ways You Can Get Better
Results Through Others

Also, you must not commit the error of putting tags on those reporting to you, such as designating a subordinate as one who will
be an accountant all his life, another as never more than a first-
level manager, and another as one lacking in creative potential and
without the capacity to develop this ability. To make sure that you
don't underestimate the human potential of those reporting to you:

1. Let your subordinates know that you expect them to be superior
   performers.
2. Remember that you hold your position of authority as a steward-
   ship which can be recalled if you handle your power unwisely.
3. Use your best judgment in allowing each subordinate a maximum
   amount of choice in the way he carries out his job assignment with
   full accountability.
4. The use of judgment in communicating with people can be important to your success with others.

Some Ways to Encourage the Growth
of More Cooperative Subordinates

As you work with people, you must remember that Rome was not
built in a day and neither will your on-the-job success base. Your
more important responsibilities are won by the way you apply effective management techniques to exercise your directional duties.
You become a better manager through a greater knowledge of principles, your own attitude toward your job, experience with trials
and errors, your sensitivity and perception, plus self-discipline.

In a refrigerator-manufacturing operation, the superintendent,
Frank Yost, had two general foremen, Will Stone and Smith Urter,
reporting to him. One of this factory's volume retailers, Clearway,
Inc., of a southern city, began receiving complaints from customers
about faulty operating units. Clearway's mechanics found short-
circuited wires, damaged sockets, loose connections, and misassem-

bled tube groupings. These deficiencies were about evenly divided between crews supervised by the general foremen.

The superintendent was a manager of long experience, so he gave some thought as to how he should handle this situation to obtain the best results. Following his thoughtful analysis, he called Will Stone into the office and gave him a real "chewing out" for allowing his quality to drop with the resulting direct and intangible sales-loss costs. Then he dismissed a fired-up Will by directing him to work out a coordinated plan for improving his quality and repairing the faulty units delivered to customers. Frank followed his conference with Will immediately by having a private session with Smith Urter. The superintendent, however, took an entirely different tone in this talk than he did with Will. He was calm with no storming or hard words. Instead he very factually reviewed the information he had about the way their refrigerators operated, pointed out that he had discussed the problem with Will, and that naturally it was to everyone's advantage to quickly satisfy the customers' complaints. The superintendent went so far as to suggest that it might be practical to send some factory men into the field, return some units to the factory, and replace some entirely. Smith was excused with instructions to work with Will on a general recovery plan to be effective as soon as possible.

The results were as Frank Yost had anticipated because the two general foremen diligently applied their different management talents to this problem. A joint plan was submitted to and approved by Frank which included reimbursing the dealers for repair costs, sending factory men to the field, returning some refrigerators, and a tightening of inspection in the factory.

Worthy of special note is the judgment and personal control which the superintendent used in passing out corrective suggestions. In each instance the method and words used were tailored to the receiving manager's particular temperament. You must remember that all people are individuals. They respond to those management methods which carry their personal appeal stamp.

You can get the kind of support which Frank Yost received by hard study, diligent work, and meaningful reviewed experiences.

Establish Your Priorities

I recently heard a plant general manager charge his subordinate, "You don't need to worry about headquarter's officials. Just keep me happy." This is a boss setting up a concrete target for his subordinate.

Most managers are convinced that a totem-pole order of important things to do is vital to success in their jobs. You will probably also agree that usually what is essential, and when it should be handled, is not as simple and clean-cut as the general manager's spelling out what he considered the first duty of his subordinate. Thus, how to pick what should be done first is an area in which managers must use effective techniques.

As a general guide, you should remember that in your opportunity system the controlling element is the customer. A retailer ordinarily finds he can get by simply through satisfying the purchaser of his goods. The same is true with the lawyer and his client, the doctor and his patient. But as a professional manager you have at least five customers—namely, your boss, your subordinates, associates, suppliers, and the ultimate purchaser of your goods or services. Thus you must exercise careful judgment as you decide which of these customers gets the first call on your limited time.

How to Go for the Payoff Punches

Sports writers are fond of interviewing champions following a winning performance. Invariably the hero explains in detail how it happened. For instance, the boxer noticed that his opponent took extra precautions to protect his eyes, dropped his left shoulder just before swinging with a hard right, was noticeably slow in backing away from sharp left jabs, came out of the clinches with both arms down at his sides. Thus the winner used his judgment, experience, know-how, and calculated risks to swing with his payoff punches. He studied, thought, estimated, and applied his specially developed skills in getting the greatest return from his payoff.

As a manager, you can't personally choose the rivets and bolts which the mechanic installs in an assembly; neither can you actually check the detail work of each person reporting to you for quality. You are not expected to select the material used in your products, handle the company's public relations, or take every worthwhile civic job which comes your way. You will as an ambitious manager find some way to handle a representative sampling of these projects, but you will not spread yourself so thin that you are unable to deliver on the duties which you must handle.

In a large manufacturing plant in New Jersey, Sid Jeffery, the engineer in charge of structural design, was advanced to the chief engineer's spot in charge of his entire department. The new chief experienced these difficulties:

1. An actual homesickness because he wasn't able to see new designs take shape on the drawing board and follow their development.

2. Missed the satisfaction of whipping out a slide rule and figuring the stress on a brand-new structure.

3. Avoided knuckling down to the knotty points of policy having to do with an overall shortage of engineers.

4. Encouraged his former subordinates to bring all their problems on structures to him for decisions.

5. Tried to establish his position by attending all the engineering report meetings, the trade sessions evenings and Saturdays, and personally preparing all his technical papers and speeches.

6. Tried to demonstrate that he was an expert in all fields, including specialized details as well as general operating practices.

Evaluate Sid's method of handling his job by checking these true-false statements:

	True	False
1. The chief engineer was an indispensable man to his department.	____	____
2. His knowledge of structures could be valuable to the company.	____	____
3. Sid's interest in detail can be an asset.	____	____

True *False*

4. Subordinates will grow under this type of management.   ____ ____

5. The output of the engineering department will be slowed down under Sid's management.   ____ ____

6. Sid needs some careful guidance from his superiors.   ____ ____

Answers: (1) false (2) true (3) true (4) false (5) true (6) true.

The chief engineer's boss, Otto Stilk, naturally was observing his new appointee's performance and, after about two months, sat down with him for an intensive review of his results. The superior commended Sid for his energy and attention to the job but quickly moved to the subject of developing the people reporting to him. (1) Otto enumerated a half dozen standout young engineers to whom Sid should be giving special attention. (2) Sid was advised to provide some challenging learning opportunities for his key employees and to move some of the structures people into electronics, electrical systems, and experimental. (3) The boss proposed to his subordinate that he let go of such chores as attending all meetings and approving the solutions to detailed problems. (4) Otto insisted that Sid take some chances by putting the decision pressure on to bring his better engineers along faster.

By such actions, Otto was insisting that Sid go for the payoff punch, which is frequently required when a manager looks at his job too narrowly. You get your rewards by accepting full directional responsibilities, by working to improve your management methods, and in developing the people reporting to you.

You should make it a part of your kit of professional management tools to always have something left to meet the unexpected or emergency job needs. By developing subordinates, you are putting money in the bank against the day when you'll need to give all your attention to some important new project, or when an opportunity for a promotion comes along for which you want to swing your full payoff punch.

How to Avoid Being Misled

Don't dodge unpleasant facts. Subordinates like to tell managers what they want to hear, and many superiors listen for only good news.

A staff manager, Roland Welch, promised his boss that some selected, detailed, personnel information would be collected from eight separate departments and made available for the superior's study within three weeks. The job of securing the details needed was delegated to David Rosen, an experienced subordinate, with careful directions that it must be ready well before the promised deadline.

Roland asked David intermittently about the progress of the assignment. He received some answering alibis about minor difficulties which the superior had corrected, and the subordinate kept assuring his boss that the information would be available when it was required. Time went by and David took a week of scheduled vacation just at the time the report was due. Before going, the subordinate left a written report to Roland in which he enumerated his many problems, which didn't cover up the fact that the assignment had not been completed. All the vital details still had to be collected. Too late, Roland realized that he should have:

1. Been more alert to the evidences that the problem was not getting handled.
2. Personally checked his subordinate's progress.
3. Made a better selection of a subordinate to work on the important assignment.
4. Been on guard against his natural tendency to look for only good news.

To build your winning base, you must remember that the payoff goes to the manager who gets results. It is a mechanism not affected by human passion or concerns; it is hard and impersonal. So one of the basic lessons you must learn as a leader is to control your own feelings as you make decisions. You must recognize that not all news can be good, expect some setbacks, and be suspicious of a subordinate who is unwilling to give you the facts even though they are unpleasant.

How to Turn Troubles into Assets

Most experienced managers have been confronted at one time or another with this directive from their boss, "Cut your overhead." This usually means, "Get some of your employees off the payroll." And this can be one of your biggest headaches because: (1) It is going to be a blow to those thrown out of work. (2) Your whole staff will be shaken up. (3) You will be expected to maintain the same production rate.

Faced with this problem, you must not lose your perspective. This is really a challenge to your ability as a leader, and one of your best actions in meeting this emergency is to rely upon your skill in communications. An honest explanation will get the best results in this disagreeable situation.

Some of the educational benefits which result from this kind of difficulty are:

1. You tighten up your organization and eliminate some problems which will become greater as time passes.

2. Employees have a more realistic appreciation of what is expected of them in their assignments.

3. Your personal qualities as a communicator are tested. Getting the facts over to another person is a skill that must be developed to a high degree if you are to build a solid base in your chosen profession.

4. You are forced to learn more about the details of your management responsibility. Such knowledge should suggest new ideas and improved methods of operating.

As you wrestle with the difficulties in using your system's secret weapon, you'll be growing as an effective manager.

SUMMARY

1. Gear your thinking to the education explosion.

2. Be selective in getting and using information.

3. Get all the benefits of training and education for:

   (a) Company
   (b) Associates
   (c) Employees.

4. Think out the job to be done.

5. Some secret weapon "do's":

   (a) Act on your own decisions.
   (b) Worry less and work more.
   (c) Make use of the initiative of those reporting to you.
   (d) Establish priorities.
   (e) Save something for the payoff punches.

6. Two secret weapon "don'ts":

   (a) Dodge unpleasant facts.
   (b) Let your troubles get you down.

NOTES TO CHAPTER 3

[1] First National City Bank, *Monthly Economic Letter* (August, 1965), p. 95.

[2] Charles P. Randall, re-ed., "Education—An Investment in People," Chamber of Commerce of the United States of America, 1964, pp. 2-11.

[3] First National City Bank, *Monthly Economic Letter* (August, 1965), p. 92.

[4] J. Frank Gaston, ed., "Patterns of Economic Growth" (San Francisco), National Industrial Conference Board (September, 1965), p. 54.

[5] "Europe Takes a Tip—from U. S. Businessmen," from a copyrighted article in *U. S. News & World Report,* January 16, 1967, p. 72.

4

Ten Ways to Turn
Yourself On

General David Sarnoff was asked, "Can a success story such as yours be repeated?" And he replied, "It can not only be repeated, it can be excelled. . . . Certainly I give the greatest measure of credit for such success as I may have achieved to the opportunity this country provided—greater than any other country in the world, in my judgment, and I have been around a good deal. A man can achieve success here regardless of his beginning or his background or his race or religion. The freedom to express whatever forces you

65

may be endowed with or are able to develop is the most precious thing an individual can have. It is worth fighting for and dying for." [1]

He also pointed out that you must be ready to make lemonade out of the lemons such as he was handed in 1930. At this time the Government had ordered RCA to separate from General Electric and Westinghouse, its parents. In addition, a worldwide depression was just getting underway; the stock market had fallen apart. Like Sarnoff—through ingenuity, wit, and effort—you can always find a way to go over, under, or around whatever happens to be your immediate crisis. When lack of sales are the difficulty, you can still find ways to sell. In fact, good managers are always selling products, services, themselves.

How to Hone Your Selling Talents

In our customer-oriented economy, the buyer pays your wages along with the returns to all employees; carries the interest on capital; and supplies reinvestment funds, rents, and profits. Thus selling is one of the most important functions of your management system. So, whatever your job assignment, improving your sales power will assist you in becoming a better manager.

You can learn some lessons from Ned Carrier's experiences. Ned, a young man with about ten years of junior management experience in a large factory, decided to try his luck as an on-the-road salesman for a manufacturer of signs sold directly to the using customers. These signs were of standard design with interchangeable panels which permitted advertising a variety of products. Additional sales were made of novel, original signs manufactured to order.

Ned Carrier was paid a liberal commission, had an unlimited territory, located his own leads, evaluated the jobs, and set prices on any specialty signs. From this tough sales assignment, he developed a self-questioning technique which you should consider practicing on your job:

Sales Aids

		Applicable	Not Applicable
1.	Am I working hard and smart?	___	___
2.	How can I improve my personal impression on the customer?	___	___
3.	Do I clearly understand what I am working for?	___	___
4.	How can I help solve the customers' problems?	___	___
5.	What's my competition?	___	___
6.	Does the prospect actually want what I'm selling?	___	___
7.	What specific improvement do I see as possible for my potential customer?	___	___
8.	Do I have a plan that has a good chance of success?	___	___
9.	Why should the customer buy?	___	___
10.	What past achievement can I point out?	___	___
11.	Does he have a weakness I can help him correct?	___	___
12.	What is the "best-foot-forward" approach?	___	___
13.	What plan is best to help me organize my own personal method of benefiting from my experience—record, study, remember?	___	___
14.	Was my prejudgment of the buyer correct?	___	___
15.	What actions or facts seemed most helpful?	___	___
16.	The usefulness of selected, effective helps, such as pictures, figures, prestige-users, diagrams?	___	___

By carefully selecting and answering the appropriate questions from this list, you can improve your salesmanship and build a stronger base as a successful manager.

Ned Carrier found that by studying himself and evaluating his total skills, he could make more sales, earn more money, become more confident in his own abilities, and increase the pleasure he experienced in his job. However, Ned quickly discovered that he had only gone part way in developing his sales ability. He found he had to keep his experiences working for him.

How to Make the Best Use of Your Persuaders

As Ned traveled around and talked with small and large businessmen, he found that each prospect had his own particular quirks, bias, and characteristics, but they all exhibited a common interest in how Ned's product might help them.

You'll find that people under your direction also have a question about how your guidance helps them, so a study of this checklist will put you in a better position to use your persuasive powers.

Help Yourself by Helping Others

	Will Work	*Not Worthwhile*
1. Endeavor to convince the person you want to influence that you have his interest in mind.	____	____
2. Make use of sincere compliments.	____	____
3. Be alert to evidences of the other person's fears.	____	____
4. Sharpen your skill in asking the right questions.	____	____
5. Strike a spark.	____	____
6. Assist in overcoming a weakness.	____	____
7. Give the other person an opportunity to sell himself.	____	____

You would not be in a position to exercise this opportunity to fill a manager's job without having displayed an ability to persuade, so refine this skill by: (1) not overgeneralizing about the capabilities of the employees under your direction, (2) cultivating your sensitivities and sharpening your look-in on others, and (3) determining what each key subordinate expects from his job.

Some specific tips to get your persuader going:

1. Earn respect by:
   (a) Knowing your job.
   (b) Giving subordinates a fair break.
   (c) Expressing your appreciation for good work.
2. Don't kill initiative by acting mean-tough.
3. Find ways to spend more time developing people.
4. Welcome the contributions of your subordinates.
5. When a decision is required, don't express uncertainty. Call the shot and be off.
6. Encourage subordinates to think about job problems.
7. Make sure job goals are understandable.
8. Don't let problems grow through neglect.
9. Treat employees as mature adults. Correct mistakes and fix responsibilities in a straightforward, tactful fashion.

As you use better persuasive salesmanship to strengthen your foundation for a more effective career in management, be alert to handicapping difficulties and dangerous pitfalls.

How to Handle the Something-for-Nothing Guys

The people who work in your department, unit, group, section, or plant are representative of a cross section of the total society. Thus you will find a small percentage who are inclined to feel that they are entitled to whatever they can filch without paying for it. These are the employees who take advantage of a soft supervisor, consistently dodge doing their share of the work, cause discipline problems, and can reduce the efficiency and morale of your crew. Under such circumstances, you must take firm control. Keep an open mind and don't condemn a subordinate until he has refused every opportunity to shape up. Your own attitude should be openly confident, expressing a certainty that you are expecting full cooperation.

You can get some specific ideas about how the feelings of others relate to your operation from a study the General Electric Company released in 1967. This exercise defines the results of some employee behavioral research which gives several useful insights into workers' reactions to selected management methods. The study was made to find out what encourages an employee to really care about how well he does his job. These are the results:

1. Productive motivation was higher where employees had some discretionary responsibility in their jobs. This right of self-determination was such a strong incentive that in spite of the unfavorable hours on second shift and the larger proportion of newer, younger employees, they had a more favorable work attitude than first-shift employees because second-shift employees had a say-so in handling their jobs.

2. Productive motivation was lower for employees in highly repetitive jobs.

3. Occasional rotation of work shifts was the poorest productive motivator—even worse than no rotation—seemingly because of the uncertainty and disappointment of expectations. Regular rotation was significantly better than occasional.

4. Greater productive motivation was found to be associated with the higher levels of activity and physical movement (walking, lifting, changing positions). This higher degree of involvement seemed to result in a feeling of accomplishment and of self-importance.

5. This study established that most direct-labor employees can be motivated to become more involved in their work with resulting better production by:

1. Allowing them to participate in the establishment of meaningful work goals.

2. The actual implementation of these goals.

3. Improved orientation, such as plant tours, meetings with managers and specialists to discuss how each job contributes to and affects the production process, emphasizing the specific importance of each job.

4. Formal job training for shop employees.

All these stimulators were specific and designed to highlight the importance of each job and its relationship to the work of others.[2]

So, before you label any of the people reporting to you as "something-for-nothing guys," be sure that you, as an effective manager, are doing everything you should:

1. To help your subordinates become job-involved.

2. To permit as much personal job determination as possible.

3. To introduce variety into jobs as appropriate.

4. To help employees feel some sense of accomplishment and personal importance.

How to Meet the Rumor Mongers

"Recent studies conducted to find out the relative effectiveness of various media reveal some interesting data. The speediest disseminator of information according to one study is the grapevine, mentioned by 38 percent as the means by which they (the employees) would most likely get the word first. Next highest mention was supervisor with 27 percent, followed by official memo, 17 percent. Bulletin boards drew a low 4 percent."[3]

In relating these facts to your job, you should be aware that gossip and visiting among employees is probably the most costly production wrecker in modern business. The only reason that there is any question of the place of social conversation on the waste totem pole is because a correct estimate of the amount of time spent in this fashion is impossible to determine. However, most experienced managers will generally agree that:

1. Some normal pleasantries between associated employees is necessary.

2. The type of work should govern how much of such interchange is justified.

3. Too much time is consumed by idle, unproductive talk.

4. Control of such waste by management edict is likely to do more harm than good.

5. Individually exercised judgment and self-control by each employee offers the most practical solution to this problem situation.

An unexpected cut in production schedules, the sudden transfer of a popular manager, an unheralded drive to cut costs or improve quality, a layoff of employees—these carry the elements of blabbing seeds. Bad news travels much more rapidly than good.

While all gossip-prone problems are not this clear-cut, as a manager preparing your solid leadership base you must accept a responsibility for providing some solutions to such efficiency-deterrent tattling. When you trace such abuses to their source, you'll find the basic answers will generally be:

1. A lack of straightforward communications. In many large organizations, this problem is recognized; but because several echelons of management interpret and pass on information both from the top downward and from the workman upward, the chances of distortion multiply. The members of management in many large companies are reluctant to change the familiar, long-established, hierarchical, level-by-level relating of instructions and information down the line. This can be out of step with today's high-speed business system.

2. That the manager, in keeping with the tempo of the times, must be able to say *yes* and *no*. He must be a real leader. He must listen to people, encourage the development of employees, set and meet targets, and organize and provide the needed ingredients for efficient output.

3. That you must find a way to deal directly in a leader-follower relationship. The management pyramid can provide the leadership which our system requires if each level can overcome the handicaps of misinformation, lack of personal involvement, buck-passing, and shortage of aids to persuasive skills. If this course fails, the familiar triangular organization must flatten out so that fewer managers carry the ultimate responsibility for securing the needed output.

4. That a need exists for real delegation. You must be a strong leader if you are to attract and hold people who have the qualities necessary to meet problems and take actions required to counteract rumor termites and myths.

How to Frustrate the "Againsters"

One of the ways that you can turn on your management powers is to accept the fact that certain individuals like to attract attention to themselves by opposing things. The more quickly you can recognize such people in your crew, the better your chances of meeting and solving this problem.

For instance, when your accident records go up, some sorehead is quick to sound off that management is only interested in profits and is saving money on proper protective equipment for the employees. In silencing the againsters, you've got to do your homework. For instance, when your accident rate goes up you must find out *why*. Is it newly hired employees? Is it foot injuries, falls, burns, back strains, machines? Look at the records and determine causes; then answer the complaints. In a midwestern foundry, these accidents happened in one week: one employee broke an arm, another sprained an ankle, and still another suffered severe abrasions of the knees and hands. Each injury was due to a fall while running in the plant to get to the time clock first at the end of their shift. Two electricians worked on a hot line without pulling the fuses and were severely burned. These five employees all violated clearly established plant rules and accounted for that week's accidents. You should use this information to stop the professional againsters.

Some Benefits You Can Gain by Meeting Chronic "Againsters" Head-On:

1. Demonstrate the manager's courage, knowledge, and ability to communicate. Help him earn the respect of employees reporting to him.

2. It will show the chronic complainers and agitators the mettle of the manager, and his logical actions will tend to discourage future irresponsible statements from uninformed would-be complainers.

3. Future, upcoming, destructive propagandists will have a harder time getting employees to accept their criticisms.

4. Employees will be encouraged to bring their questions directly to the manager rather than accept the agitator's words.

5. This will result in the kind of success experience which gives the manager the confidence he needs to handle even more difficult problems.

6. This action will tend to create a better working atmosphere throughout the manager's section. It clears the air and promotes a better understanding.

As you consider the values of confrontation with the troublemaking againsters, you must remember that there is always more than one way to solve any management problem. When, in your judgment, the effect upon the individual, the total group, and on the results you want to obtain will be better served, let the against propose a solution to the problem. Such an action:

1. Takes you out of a defensive role and opens an aggressive, new avenue for a conclusion of the difficulty.

2. Is the best way to fully involve the dissenting employee in productive work and possibly even obtain his cooperation.

3. Is one of the best ways to tell a subordinate that you know he is important.

4. Gives the employee an opportunity to show that only he has and can make use of his very special talents. This is his chance to show up the boss.

5. Is likely to add a new touch of excitement to the job. It can stimulate an employee with a lackadaisical attitude to change until he actually enjoys his work.

Avoid the Deadening "Thing-to-Do" Kind of Managing

As you strive to build your solid career base, remember to turn on your management powers. You can't be like everyone else. You have to be a distinct personality.

Wilt Surim, chief industrial planner of Sepoy Manufacturing Company, told the plant manager, Ward Baker, that one of their big problems in the plant was caused by production superintendent

Steve Chemal who would not yell even when he was getting hurt. Ward naturally asked him what he meant. Wilt explained, "Seventy per cent of his shop orders come to him already behind schedule, but he's not going to complain because it's not the thing to do. In the first place, Steve wants to be a nice guy, not get anyone else in trouble. Second, he always has a ready-made alibi for underperformance by his shop. Also, he's had enough experience to know that if he solves a problem he'll have to work on others which are unknown and, thus, more difficult. So, for these reasons, he just lets things drift."

Ward commended Wilt for detecting the superintendent's slide downward toward conformity, saying that Steve had probably not realized what was happening and that he would get him straightened out.

Score yourself on how well you recognize the dangers which you must guard against in following the line group conformity expressed by the "in" thing to do:

		O.K.	Watch
1.	A way of performing a job that hasn't changed in a long time.	___	___
2.	Rigid-thinking managers in key spots slowing down your progress toward everyday excellence.	___	___
3.	A "they"-do-it-this-way or an "everybody"-thinks-this-is-the-right-answer kind of decision.	___	___
4.	Being convinced on your own that a particular course is the right way to go.	___	___
5.	Using a special effort to make sure you get a balanced informational picture.	___	___
6.	Highly structured organizational procedures and policy controls which stall your personal right of choice.	___	___
7.	Well thought-out individual decisions which will usually be beneficial to your company's goals.	___	___
8.	Uncomfortable group pressures which naturally tend to arise against a different way of doing things proposed by a creative manager.	___	___
9.	Self-confidence built by careful study, experience, and a knowledge that forward thinkers have always been subjected to opposition.	___	___

Acceptable answers: (1) watch (2) watch (3) watch (4) O.K. (5) O.K. (6) O.K. (7) O.K. (8) watch (9) O.K.

It is only by expressing your own individuality that you can truly turn on your management powers and make sure that you don't drift into being a "thing-to-do" kind of operating manager.

Always Be the Real You

Another important stone in your management career foundation is that of gaining the favorable acceptance of others.

The owner of the Plumb Line Toolmaking Shop in South Chicago was a strong-minded individualist named Martin Snider. One of his key employees was a young graduate mechanical engineer named Stephen Harick who had three years' experience as a toolmaker.

In the upcoming local election, Martin was a strong supporter of X individual for the city commission. Stephen made no bones about the fact that he was using his spare time to help Y get elected rather than X for the commission seat to be filled.

The shop owner smiled upon his young subordinate's efforts in a patronizing sort of way—until X lost the election. Then he turned upon Stephen in disappointed bitterness, blaming him for the defeat of his candidate.

The young toolmaker quit on the spot, telling his boss that no job was worth that kind of guff. Before the day was out, Stephen had a couple of job offers. However, he thought this was the time to try his luck with his own shop. So, with the help of his local banker, he raised the money to start a small, quality toolmaking operation.

Stephen, through his know-how and small overhead costs, was the low bidder on a complex, very close-tolerance die. It so happened that Martin needed a number of these special tools to win a very lucrative contract for the Plumb Line Toolmaking Shop. So the former employer was forced by the pressures of good business to eat a little crow, buy the tools from his former employee, and help his competitor succeed.

Here are five good management foundation facts you can learn from the Plumb Line Toolmaking Shop episode:

1. Stephen gained by being himself.

2. Martin's loss shows what can happen when a manager steps reck-
    lessly into the sensitive areas of politics. In this same emotion-
    packed category, you should put "religion" and "women."

3. People value their rights of self-expression and personal opinion.

4. You should use your authority with judgment.

5. By being yourself, you can:

    (a) Win a place of profit and distinction.

    (b) Make your greatest contribution to the total company and
         job progress.

You'll get better on-the-job results if you try to avoid startling
your subordinates with sudden out-of-character actions. The people
reporting to you want you to be predictable; so, as you make
improvements in your management methods, remember that these
changes must be directly related to your being yourself. This
will affect the speed and solidarity with which you establish your
credibility.

How You Can Gain by Admitting Your Errors

Charles Warden, the plant general manager of the QRT Co.,
factory equipment builders, held a meeting of his executive committee to discuss why they had missed in bidding too high on a
profitable contract. Present at this review were the managers in
charge of sales, top finance, engineering, and manufacturing. After
an extended discussion, it came out that the engineering manager
was the only member of the committee who knew that an expensive
burner and exhaust fan at the end of each boiler was not a part
of the bid package. He had learned this fact by talking with the
customer. The other committee members had been misled because
a draftsman had shown the completed assembly, including burner
and fan, on the drawing for information purposes.

After listening to some weak alibis, Charles Warden said, "Here
are a couple of things we are going to do right now. First, a copy of
every request for bid will be sent to each of us. Second, before the
final price is quoted, we will have a review by this group of our costs

and profit expectations with supplemental charts and diagrams." Then the general manager added, "As you have ideas which will prevent this kind of thing from happening again, let me have them. That's all for now."

This boiler-bid fiasco shows how easily poor internal communications can cause serious trouble.

Here are some benefits which the QRT Co. and its top management organization obtained because their general manager quickly admitted the error and his part in it:

1. The boss was in a much better position to nail down the short-comings of his subordinates.

2. The general manager was forced to use restrained and more equitable punishment in correcting his key supporters in the organization.

3. An emergency procedure was quickly devised to prevent the recurrence of this serious error.

4. This essential management group was brought more closely together by the evident need for better exchange of information.

5. Because managers and employees alike recognize that it takes courage to admit an error, the QRT Co. general manager gained some special and valuable respect from the people reporting to him.

So, to turn on your management powers and firm up your success base, take mistakes in stride and have a do-better-next-time attitude.

Some Costs of Apple-Polishing

The QRT Co. managers had a healthy respect for each other. This is not always true because some individuals in a management organization seek personal advantage through pretense and artificial or real overservility. "Bootlickers" and "yes-men" come in every hue and degree from the true hero worshiper to the synthetic who eagerly indicates, "Just let me find out what the boss thinks, and I'm for it."

You can seldom be absolutely sure whether a subordinate fits properly at one end of the apple-polishing scale or the other; and it's not necessary that you should since, wherever the management parasite is located, he's the bad apple that spoils the barrel. He is harmful to himself, to his superior, and to the organization.

For instance, Mr. Van Lor, the Radairy Company president, an appliance manufacturer with about 400 employees, asked his staff assistant to look over his proposed annual speech to all management. Despite the fact the staff man was not favorably impressed with the speech—since it contained many pompous comments which pictured Van Lor as an egotistical, "do-it-all-myself" kind of manager—he told his boss that he thought the material was excellent.

What's wrong with this kind of apple-polishing? A good subordinate has an obligation to try to help his boss. By being a supine "yes-man," the staff man hurts *himself* by:

1. Destroying his own self-respect. This dishonesty leaves a mark. He can't enjoy his work and must be tense and constantly on guard.

2. Misleading himself. He obviously believed that this was the way to get along; but the next superior whom he serves may be a sure-enough leader and interested in getting some real support from his subordinate. Such a manager will quickly reduce this assistant's position.

3. Denying himself the value of the mental exercise which he must get if he is to become a strong manager and reap real rewards through the proper use of effective management techniques.

The *superior* loses because:

1. He was denied a chance to make his best impression since his subordinate was afraid to give him the facts as he saw them.

2. His future was handicapped because he received no hint of his serious overegotism, as well as the technical shortcomings of his communications, which if not improved will catch up with him.

3. He'll get himself into much worse trouble than just a bad speech, because he is insulated from reactions upward through the organization.

The *company* loses by:

1. The poorer teamwork engendered by Mr. Lor's unfortunate speech.

2. The distorted picture of management which the average employee of this firm will get.

3. The misleading pattern which is set for other members of management which can lead them to believe this is the way to succeed in their jobs.

There are some practical ways to avoid these costs.

How to Use Honesty with Kindness

Mr. Van Lor of the Radairy Company was led into a problem situation because he lacked an honest and forthright subordinate who would give him this kind of answer:

1. "Sir, you'll get better acceptance if you take a 'we' attitude. Remember that most of us want to feel *with* you—that we have a part in your success."

2. "I've changed some of your words around, staying with your ideas. You may notice it's a little shorter. Remember, it's going to be a long evening. A good, snappy, punchy, meaty couple or so of thoughts such as you have here will have these managers going out of the annual dinner meeting with their chests expanded— proud of their company, their own part in its operation, and its vigorous, lay-it-on-the-line top management."

This subordinate is using a skilled, critical technique you'll do well to study. Note these elements:

1. He's being honest.
2. He's doing his correcting in a kind and intelligent fashion.
3. He's giving Mr. Lor all the credit he can in keeping with the need to be truthful and sincere.
4. He's making an appeal to the boss' natural desire for harmony and unity of purpose.

If you handle your important contacts with your boss, peers, and subordinates in accordance with these principles, *you'll* not have to tell others about your credibility—they'll see it in the best possible light.

SUMMARY

1. Work at being a better salesman by:

   (a) Preparing yourself.

   (b) Making the best use of your strengths.

2. Practice being a better persuader.

3. Learn how to handle these handicapping difficulties:

   (a) The something-for-nothing guys.

   (b) The rumor mongers.

   (c) The professional "againsters."

   (d) Becoming the thing-to-do kind of manager.

4. Gain the favorable acceptance of others by:

   (a) Being yourself.

   (d) Admitting errors.

   (c) Avoiding apple-polishing.

   (d) Using honesty with kindness.

[1] General David Sarnoff, "Envisioning the Future," *Nation's Business* (© June, 1966), pp. 68-70.

[2] Dr. Melvin Sorcher, "Motivating the Hourly Employee," Behavioral Research Service, Personnel and Industrial Relations Services, General Electric, 1967.

[3] Eugene Walton, "Communicating Down the Line: How They Really Get the Word," *Personnel* (July-August, 1959), pp. 78-82.

II

HANDLE YOUR PRESENT JOB
TO ADVERTISE YOUR ABILITY

5

How to Listen
When Money Talks

My experience has convinced me that to get ahead you must: (1) advertise your results-getting ability, and (2) develop your performance talents and skills. In practicing effective management techniques, you'll give your stock a boost if you master the use of money, jobs, supply, demand, price, and forge-ahead drive.

Money speaks three languages: as a storage of wealth, a standard of value, and a medium of exchange. You can promote yourself if you listen well when money talks.

How You Gain by Keeping Your Capital Assets Moving

"James J. Ling, the glib and agile chairman of Dallas' Ling-Temco-Vought, Inc., is a student of chess and military tactics who practices the art of the breakthrough with consummate skill. At a time when tight money was preventing some businessmen from even building a new plant, Ling borrowed $80 million to buy control of Chicago-based Wilson & Co., Inc., whose nearly $1 billion in sales made it more than double the size of his own company.

" 'The Wilson take-over will go down as one of the most deftly handled business coups of our time' says one awed Wall Street investment banker." [1]

Whereas a thief stole Silas Marner's hoarded money Mr. Ling is using the same commodity to build a fast-growing corporate empire of largely unrelated types of companies, but all returning a profit.

When you think of money as a storage of wealth, remember these rules:

1. Inflation during the 30 years ending in 1966 has averaged 2.2 per cent annually—which means that money buried a generation ago would have lost well over half its value in purchasing power.

2. Just to stay even, you and your company must earn a return on your capital investment equal to the inflation percentage.

3. Costs over which you have the most control are: (a) efficient use of material, (b) labor, and (c) reasonable inventory.

4. Sales supply the return to meet all costs and earn profits in your business.

5. You must keep your capital turning over. If you use half as much money and see that it goes twice as fast through your business, you will get a return equal to the doubled amount.

6. When wealth is used to stimulate a dynamic organization, employees show more enthusiasm for their work. They are proud to be a part of a growing company—one which is going ahead.

7. In choosing between valuable men and valuable products, men are most important. Andrew Carnegie said that if you took away his money and his mills but left him his keymen, within ten years he would have his mills and his money back again. Thus, employees, as a storage of wealth, must be encouraged to use their full talents.

How to Build the Personal Assets in Your Storehouse

Only a select few managers are directly involved in acquiring the original money capital to launch a business at the start. Most managers are concerned with their success in an established business organization.

In this situation, you can make the greatest contribution to your company's storage of wealth by working through the people reporting to you. To do this properly, you must not hesitate to let your good manager qualities shine; let your job knowledge and current performance clearly reflect your get-things-done qualities.

As you build your career to meet these requirements, the first essential is that you convince yourself that you want to be a manager. Only you can make this decision by studying the benefits and values, and then weighing them against the tensions, efforts, and uncertainties of this demanding profession. A second requirement is: Don't hesitate to move from one company to another, one line of business to another, or into entirely different work. Your success must be characterized by mobility. As early as you can find the kind of job that you most want to do, settle there. You shouldn't jump around like a frog, in and out of first one job and then another, but use your measured judgment. Don't worry about others' opinions.

After you have fully committed yourself to the profession of management, then work on building up the people under your direction. It is only by developing outstanding subordinates that you can fully advertise your own superiority as a professional manager. Aim for the top, which means that you must have competent people to fill your present spot.

As you work to help others become managers, remember:

(1) Don't be hampered by any artificial, intellectual, or social caste barriers. One of the strongest, repeatedly proven axioms of American business is that regardless of which side of the tracks you may call home, it is not a restriction on your success as a manager. In a survey of 239 major industrial firms to determine the specialized experience of the men who served as presidents of these large corporations, William P. Dommermuth concludes that, "Perhaps the most

significant finding is that the presidency typically goes to a man who has spent the great majority of his career in one field and who has risen through a series of positions in that field. This implies that he had to prove his mettle in a succession of increasingly difficult assignments in some area of business operation. In the process, he developed and demonstrated his executive abilities. In the light of all this, it might be most reasonable to conclude that the odds of becoming corporate president, while not entirely unrelated to the field of past service, seem to be largely the creation of the individual, his capabilities, and his performance in whatever field he has chosen." [2]

(2) You should encourage formal education which has intrinsic as well as advertising value. To stay in the competitive race for success in your profession, get your share of the available education and help subordinates do the same.

(3) Make it clear to those reporting to you that in our business society personal performance continues to be the unmistakable pay-off quality.

How Money Talks as a Performance Evaluator

In many business enterprises, union agreements require an automatic wage increase when the Consumer Price Index goes up. This is familiarly called a "cost-of-living" adjustment. Since World War II, the inflation spiral has followed an almost constant upward tilt, causing many employees to become accustomed to receiving at least an annual raise in pay. Such automatic increases in wages have tended to dilute the talking power of money as a motivator.

When your company is a party to such an agreement, you must accept this as one of the difficulties of administering your job. However, even when the rules require a blanket raise, you still have the leverage of merit funds which can be used to recognize special performance. To the degree possible, save your money for use as a standard-of-value motivator.

Normally, managers are not included in cost-of-living adjustments, but many will speak up if they feel the boss is neglecting their wages.

Here's a recent conversation between a top staff man, Dewey Alexis, and his plant manager, Duke Doyle. Dewey had not received any salary increase or even discussed his job performance with Duke for well over a year. So, with some concern, the staff man went to the boss' office to talk about his standing. Before Dewey could say anything, Duke Doyle charged, "You are not coming up with enough new ideas." As the subordinate was recovering from this shock, the boss continued, "Of course, we are always deficient in this area. Everyone must keep thinking. And you are *not* the only one who's guilty of this shortcoming around here; but we are going to have to tighten up and get more work out of the people on the payroll." Then, after looking intently at the subordinate, Duke said, "Give some thought to the problems you know about and tell me what we ought to do to solve them—Now, what did you have on your mind?" Dewey, with a now-or-never attitude, replied, "I came in to remind you that my rate had not been reviewed for a year, but I suppose right now is the wrong time to bring this up."

The plant manager replied in a sharp tone, "You're right in the last part of your statement, but wrong in thinking your rate has not been considered. Yep! This is the wrong time for you to bring up the question of a raise. Now, if that's all you have, I'm busy. Have to get some work done." As Dewey Alexis left the office, money was talking pretty loud to him. Duke Doyle had sent his message across to him in sledgehammer fashion.

Get More for Your Wage Dollar

Give your evaluation of the Duke-Dewey interview by checking "right" or "wrong" after each statement.

	Right	*Wrong*
1. Dewey should not have gone to Duke's office.	____	____
2. The boss used a poor method of opening the conversation.	____	____
3. When he left his superior's office, the subordinate knew where he had been falling down on the job.	____	____

Right *Wrong*

4. Dewey should have been more emphatic in making his point. —— ——

5. Duke shirked his responsibility by not informing Dewey earlier of his dissatisfaction with his work. —— ——

6. The subordinate should not have mentioned his wages when the superior carried the conversation as he did. —— ——

7. Dewey should have been more alert to his poor relationship with his boss. —— ——

8. More exchange between the two managers about who, what, why, where, and when would have helped communications. —— ——

9. The plant manager's words suggest that he thought the staff man knew where his performance was deficient. —— ——

10. The subordinate should have demanded a clearer explanation from his boss. —— ——

You'll be interested to know that Dewey Alexis resigned and joined another company immediately after this exchange with Duke Doyle.

You can get more for the wage dollar you spend for management if you work at building right relationships. Duke Doyle missed several opportunities to get more for his money.

You should have marked the ten statements: (1) wrong (2) right (3) wrong (4) right (5) right (6) wrong (7) right (8) right (9) right (10) right.

Eight correct checks is excellent.

Six correct checks is good.

Less than six means you should review the entire interview thoughtfully and carefully.

Some Ways Money Talks Best

"At the start of your career, married, with young children and a load of debts, what you need from your employer is all the current cash income and protection against death or disability you can get. What you don't need is a retirement income plan to which you are required to make fat contributions. But if you're in your late fifties, around the peak of your taxable earnings and free of many of your family burdens, what you need is assurance of a lifetime retirement income for you and your wife. What you don't need is more current cash income on which you'll pay more taxes." [3]

Many professionally managed companies have for years used deferred retirement benefits to stimulate and retain selected top executives. Options to buy company stock is another common compensation technique; however, again, this has been normally reserved for the higher levels of management.

In recent years, alert managers are tying strings to their better employees at all levels by: (1) company-maintained pension plans, (2) wage increases for seniority, (3) payroll deductions for savings bond purchases, (4) stock purchase plans, (5) savings plans in which an employee may decide to have a specified portion of his wages placed in a special account. Usually the company adds from 50 per cent to 100 per cent in matching funds for a selected number of years.

These individualized money motivators as mediums of exchange will not only help you retain your most effective employees but also create better morale and obtain greater output from more willing employees.

How to Get Better Management for Your Money

To get a real payoff when money talks, push the thinking, deciding, and acting far down in the management organization. In successfully using effective management techniques, operating decisions must be made as close as possible to the producing employees.

Such actions will put you in position to get these values: (1) Producers will have greater incentive to work harder. (2) There will be more efficient methods used, plus better utilization of people and machines. (3) A stronger management line will help you avoid costly delays. (4) Better lower-level managers will insure continued excellent management. (5) A strong first-level management is the key to unity in the organization. (6) Higher-level management can concentrate on long-range plans.

You will actually get these results if decision-makers wisely use their time. One of the most successful managers I've known said, "Time is the raw material of profit." This was his method of pointing out that the way you and others use your time spells the difference between success and failure for your company.

To improve your use of this valuable commodity, check yourself on these questions:

1. What was the most important single thing I accomplished today?

2. Why was this so significant?

3. How might I have handled it more quickly and better?

4. Will this important item be a repeater?

5. If it occurs again, how can I identify it more quickly and dispose of it more efficiently?

6. Did I dodge a job today which I should have handled?

7. Could some of the jobs I did have been done as well or better by an assistant?

8. Did I allow job pressures to get to me and spoil the quality of my work?

9. Would more thought have enabled me to get better results?

10. What do I plan to tackle the first thing tomorrow?

You can provide the greatest help to yourself and your company if you'll remember to have the manager at the working level make on-the-job decisions; keep reminding yourself about how you use the scarce commodity—time.

How to Look at Debt Without Fear

As you work to advertise your competence as a successful manager, you need to know one of the special languages of money—debt.

"Out of debt, out of danger." "Loans and debts make worries and frets." "Never spend money before you have it." Suppose these slogans were taken to be literally true and the majority of the American people followed these tenets. What would be the effect upon you?

As a get-ahead manager, you need to appreciate that:

(1) *Debts within reason are good economics.* For instance, with a backlog of orders, a needed profile milling machine which can be purchased through a bank loan can become a profitable management-judgment decision if it: (a) increased productivity and resulted in cost savings through the use of the machine which would enable your company to pay off the debt within a reasonable time; (b) enabled you to use the liquid cash retained because of the loan for possible purchase of a lucrative sales outlet which offered a once-in-a-lifetime opportunity, or some other profit-making investment.

In thinking of debts as they apply to you through personal experience, most of you either are buying or have acquired a home by paying off a mortgage. This can be good business for you because it permits you to enjoy the advantages of property ownership without waiting years to save the cash for its entire cost. Also, for most people, it results in money savings which would otherwise be used up without leaving anything to show for your hard-earned dollars.

(2) *Debts in the aggregate are different from individual obligations.* For example, statements of total debts are misleading because such figures fail to consider: (a) the effects of increasing population, (b) the fact that individuals are constantly repaying and reacquiring new debts, (c) the stimulating economic results of reasonable obligations, and (d) the composition of this total debt.

In meeting the money performance requirements of the group or unit you manage in your company, you need to apply the same tests which make sense in your personal affairs. First, your total costs must not exceed your income. Second, when you add to your promises to pay: (a) make sure you can meet interest and principal requirements, (b) expect to obtain a valuable return from your commitment, (c) determine, in your judgment, that the timing is right for assuming the obligation.

As a self-advertising manager, you will—depending upon your level in the organization—buy or recommend the purchase of the new milling machine if: (a) The acquisition will reduce your labor and/or scrap costs appreciably. (b) You think that all costs can be met. (c) You are convinced that your overall efficiency will be improved. (d) You think that the time is right to add to the capital equipment of your unit.

When viewed in this fashion, debts should not arouse unreasonable fears.

How You Can Benefit from Knowing More about Debts

Some time ago Thomas Carlyle wrote, "There are but two ways of paying debts—increase of industry in raising income, increase of thrift in laying out." As previously stated, by casually looking at the 36-year example, it would seem that our economy has not met this test.

However, in more closely examining this historical record, as a manager one of the first facts to consider is that the U. S. population has grown by an average of 2 million people per year during this period. Thus, more people share the greater debt. Some further analysis shows that in 1929 each individual's share of the total debt was $1,567.32, while in the mid-1960s it was $6,474.82. When these figures are corrected for inflation (the increase in the consumer price index is 84 per cent, 1929 compared with 1965), the individual's share of total debt actually declines to $3,518.92; and, to offset this added debt, on the average, each person has almost twice the real after-taxes income that he had in 1929.

Even this revealing bit of information is not all you need know to better understand the double personality of debts, because not only is there an owing side, but there is also an owning or investing benefit. The interest you receive on your savings account in your bank helps to offset the $10.7 billion per year increase (during the 36-year period) in individual and noncorporate debts. Next in size of increase for the same period is corporate debt at $10 billion annually. The bulk of this corporate debt money went into capital equipment, new plants, inventories, or other investment. And, as a result of these expenditures, we have greater productivity, profits, rents, and interests paid to millions of property holders. All these returns are benefits stemming from corporate debts accumulated through the years.

Federal government debts have grown by $7.1 billion as an annual average in this past 36-year period, and state and local government debts increased $2.2 billion annually on the average during this same series of years. Thus, in spite of wars, welfare boondoggling, bureaucratic inefficiencies, and heavy spending for defense in both the hot- and the cold-war periods, the greatest amount of total debt obligations has accumulated in the private sector of our economy. As a manager, you have the responsibility to see that the bulk of our total debt load pays its way. You can discharge this accountability in most instances when you, as suggested by Carlyle, "increase productivity and/or decrease costs."

How You Can Benefit from the Best Single Gauge of Performance

Albert Sanderson, general manager of a large specialty subassembly manufacturer for the automobile industry, developed a system of profit targets for each of the departments in his plant. His plan included collecting all costs, direct and indirect labor, materials, and overhead. These expenses were compared with monthly profit goals and were regularly reviewed by the general manager and the department managers.

When asked by his boss for the advantages of his system, Albert Sanderson listed: (1) Everybody understands the importance of money. (2) Profits are the goal we are all striving to reach. (3) What a manager does or does not do is reflected in the profit mirror. (4) Such an objective is a help in combining the efforts of all in united teamwork endeavor. (5) Once the formula is worked out, it is an objective measure of each group's overall performance efficiency. (6) It encourages the right kind of competition. (7) Your better managers welcome the opportunity to earn proper recognition.

The general manager's superior was so impressed with Albert's plan that it was installed in all the other plants of the company.

As a measure of the value of this Better Total Performance Method, the poorer managers soon started referring to it as "the barbecue," and the good ones declared that it was the first time their superiors had recognized and given them credit for their exceptional results.

SUMMARY

1. Remember and use the three languages which money speaks as:

   (a) A storage of wealth.

   (b) A standard of value.

   (c) A medium of exchange.

2. Keep your capital assets working for you.

3. Expand your management assets by self-development and improving subordinates.

4. Use money as an evaluator.

5. Build strength into your management line.

6. View debt in its proper perspective.

7. Learn to use money as a clear gauge of better total performance.

NOTES TO CHAPTER 5

[1] "LTV Blitzes Its Way into Ranks of Giants," *Business Week* (March 18, 1967), p. 179.

[2] William P. Dommermuth, "On the Odds of Becoming Company President," *Harvard Business Review* (May-June, 1966), p. 72.

[3] *Wichita Eagle*, July 9, 1966, p. 4B. Sylvia Porter Column, "Your Money's Worth." Courtesy Wichita Eagle and Publishers-Hall Syndicate.

6

How to Be
a Job-Maker

Your attitude toward your work, the reactions of others to you, and the judgment you use in making job assignments are a reflection of your experiences—what you have learned. However, it must be admitted that Edmund Burke had a point when he said, "You can never plan the future by the past." It is always true that one test of leadership is the ability to adjust to meet new and changed conditions.

Apply the Lessons of the Past to the Present

Hubert Stroud, a first-level manager of an assembly line manufacturing operation, had difficulty getting the parts to the proper place when they were needed. The standard remedy for this kind of problem was to hire a parts-chaser and give him the duty of expediting the needed materials.

Hubert hired an experienced and well-recommended man named Jerold Herrin for this job. However, the assembly-line schedule steadily worsened instead of improving. After talking with Jerold, the manager realized that the expeditor had no concept of what needed to be done. Further, Jerold was so discouraged that he insisted on being transferred to another job. Hubert complied with Jerold's request but was still in trouble on the assembly line and was further behind than before.

Which of these ideas do you think might have helped resolve the assembly-line shortage?

		Yes	No
1.	Hubert should have learned more about Jerold's past experience.	___	___
2.	This expeditor job required work-around creativity.	___	___
3.	The ability to get along well with others was important.	___	___
4.	Jerold should have had an opportunity to express his feelings about the parts-chaser job.	___	___
5.	Detailed instructions should have preceded the job assignment.	___	___
6.	Hubert should have found out why the assembly-line shortages came about.	___	___
7.	The manager was too quick to follow the established pattern.	___	___
8.	The line should have been stopped until the trouble was located.	___	___
9.	Hubert should have appealed to his superior for help.	___	___
10.	Jerold should have been kept on the job.	___	___

The key thought in this series of suggestions is number six. By tracing the cause, Hubert found that subassembly and the stock-room were undermanned. He was able to substantiate this with his boss. Then, by higher-level coordination, the difficulties in the sections outside Hubert's control were corrected, and the late deliveries to the assembly line cleared up right away.

Statements numbered "one" through "five" could be marked "yes," as helpful when Hubert decided to follow the plans used in the past. Number seven points out the basic fallacy; and eight, nine, and ten should be marked "no," since positive action in these areas would have weakened Hubert's leadership.

You should never blindly follow past practices without considering whether there is a better way to do the job. And one of the best helps in making a name for yourself on your job is to know as much as possible about the people reporting to you.

It Helps to Know What's Going on

While there is no substitute for knowing your subordinates as individuals, often you can avoid unpleasant surprises if you're well informed generally about what those people reporting to you will likely hold as a group opinion. For instance, your ability to get results is affected by the age of the labor force. Fifty per cent of the present labor force was not even born when our country entered World War II. Thus, on the average, every second person reporting to you has: (1) no firsthand appreciation of the frantic search for jobs which took place in the depression of the Thirties; (2) no idea of the self-help used to insure economic security in old age or for disability or sickness before government social programs were established; (3) the belief that the government can and should guarantee economic prosperity; (4) for many years lived under the National Employment Act of 1946 which President Kennedy defined as "... an historic affirmation of the responsibility of the Federal Government 'to promote maximum employment, production, and purchasing power.'"; (5) the idea that he must watch you to keep from being pushed around; (6) the idea that he is an especially important person. This notion has been nurtured by the scramble of businesses and industries to employ superior people.

As you keep these specific attitude-builders in mind, you'll be in a better position to meet some unexpected problem posed by a subordinate who fails to respond to your direction as you feel he should.

How to Use the Magic Duo

Job-making in effective management has other elements which are separate from the individual's reaction.

"For the best part of 30 years, while Stalin was running the Soviet Union like a house of correction, the job of balancing consumer demand and supply was a planner's dream simply because demand was always big enough to soak up the limited supply. Stalin's capital-investment policy, begun in 1928, wound up by allocating about half the nation's total output to the military and to industrial fixed and working capital.

"Soviet economists, proudly contemplating their resplendent supply-demand equilibrium, boasted that their economy had forever done away with overproduction, shutdowns, unemployment, and other attendant ills that were supposed to be endemic in the world of private enterprise." [1]

With the passing of Stalin on March 5, 1953, and the succession of Khrushchev, production of consumer goods expanded to the extent that the planner began to realize that guiding a Sputnik into space was child's play compared with trying to outguess a consumer given the chance to pick and choose. "Between 1950 and 1965 retail sales nearly tripled. . . . But in the same years savings-bank deposits increased nearly ten times. . . . (A Soviet official when asked to explain this said that) the main reason they (people) have been saving more than they 'should' is that they have disdained some of the goods on sale." [2]

Wrapped up in these Soviet experiences are the factors which you as a manager must remember are needed to make jobs. These essential elements are production and real demand. If you become a self-promoting manager, a true job-maker, the magic duo of output and genuine purchasing power must be in relative balance.

Leo Garson and Saul Mayberry, two management employees of a large airplane company, used their spare time to build a three-place prototype airplane. This success caused them to start a business of their own. In doing this, they brought together the needed people and convinced them of an agreeable method of organization; secured bank credit; selected key leaders for the company; provided special performance inducements for these selected people; and gave their most valued subordinates immediate and important initial responsibilities to locate and obtain tools, space, materials, and employees.

As a manager you can improve your chances for success in your job-making by applying your ability to: (1) select the right employees, see that they are properly trained for their work and correctly assigned, determine that they know what they are supposed to do, help them solve job problems, and then see that they do achieve results; (2) make the best use of materials, avoid waste, reduce costs, be alert to the possible use of more desirable substitutes; (3) keep current on the latest machines, don't let a competitor get an advantage by being the first to install a cost-cutting piece of equipment, insist on top preventive maintenance to keep machines running at peak efficiency, and be prepared to enumerate reasons why for any needed facilities. Make use of all space, study rearrangement of layout, and remember that new tools are cheap if the cost is offset by more and better production.

Even with the best management, the most efficient use of natural resources, the hard and dedicated labor of people, and the finest of continuously improved machinery, you can't create and have more and more jobs without a market. You must be able to sell your product.

In meeting this demand, remember that most of your market is interested in "Where can I get the most for my money?"

Some Built-In Benefits You Can Use

First: When most of your buyers are motivated by what they think is good for them, you can allocate your production resources and set prices with some assurance that you can earn some profits.

Second: When products go to the nonprofit sector, you as a manager must exercise greater care and better judgment because the buyers often play by a different set of rules. For instance, governments often demand a special article to do specific work, with no consideration as to whether your production costs may be excessive or if you can make a profit. Charitable institutions likewise often operate on a nonprofit, philanthropic sense of ideals.

Third: Free choice and profitable returns in the market provide an immediate feedback to you as a producer. If people don't buy, you know something is wrong and are on notice to do something about it. By contrast, in the nonprofit area returns are often too slow to be of use as an accurate guide for correction of a misjudgment in product, style, or cost.

Fourth: You don't have to please everybody. All you must do is attract enough customers to pay your total costs, needed future investments, and leave a reasonable margin for a fair return to the investor for his contribution to making your product possible.

Fifth: With the average annual improvement in productivity, coupled with increased population, more people steadily increase their dollar power in the marketplace, giving you greater opportunities for success as a job-maker in your chosen profession.

Sixth: You have the means to be of exceptional service to others. John Gray, chairman and president of Omark Industries, Inc., said, "There can be a great feeling of satisfaction in considering that the company you helped to build has created jobs for hundreds or perhaps thousands; that you are partly responsible for the good lives that are made possible by ... well-paying and interesting jobs; that the income of the company you head is contributing to comfortable homes, college educations.... To create a job is to create a livelihood for someone, and that is no small contribution." [3]

How to Put Through Improvements

To acquire these benefits, you have to continually work to better your own job performance by making changes which are not always popular.

When a new machine, tool, layout, method, or other equipment offers a better and/or less costly way to obtain greater output per man-hour worked, it's your job to see that this improvement is fully exploited. In such circumstances, you will usually encounter some resistance because jobs are changed, habits disrupted, and often some operation eliminated. You'll find it worthwhile to anticipate objections and be prepared to meet them.

Suppose you are planning to install a conveyor which will replace 20 men now using hand trucks to deliver the stock and parts needed on an assembly operation. Will you be able to use the ideas suggested on this checklist? In what order?

Some hints which can help get acceptance when a change is made:

1. Tell the employees that: "As far back as reliable data can be found ... the recent changes in types of employment and labor skills can be identified as long-term trends.... As a percentage of the total labor force ... unskilled workers have been more than cut in half." [4]

2. Explain that more things people want have come through the development and use of better machines and equipment; that changes and improvements are not new but, rather, have been continuously adding to our overall prosperity with a progressive increase in jobs. Large capital investments and almost full employment of a total labor force approaching 80 million people are convincing proof that machines make jobs rather than destroy them.

3. Be careful to express a positive, constructive, and confident attitude. Any doubts you may have about the real benefits of a change are quickly ferreted out by people reporting to you. They make it their business to know you much better than you suspect. You must be convinced yourself that the new machine, the changed method, the rearranged equipment, or whatever the hoped-for improvement, is in fact a better way to achieve efficiency on your job assignment.

4. Define some progress markers, such as more pieces with less effort or better quality accomplished through the changed procedure. Nothing attracts followers like success, so arrange to show your subordinates what can be achieved.

5. Study what concrete rewards may be built into the changed work improvement methods. It's possible that the workmen can be shown that success may mean: (a) personal recognition, (b) more

money, (c) added pensions, vacations, sick leave, or other fringe benefits, (d) that someone he respects will think well of him and tell him so.

6. Tell the employees well before the change is made. Give them a chance to blow off steam and get used to the idea before you make the change.

7. Have your plans fully thought out. Know how the change will affect each workman.

8. Answer all questions honestly and frankly.

9. Set up a schedule for installation of the change and meet it.

10. Express a willingness to listen to any proposal which might obtain better results.

11. If the protests become too strong, blame the change on orders from upstairs.

In using these hints, start with number seven. Be sure that you have reviewed all facets of the change: what the new arrangement will look like, what it will do, who will be affected, and how much displacement or change of established routine will occur. Ask yourself who will raise the strongest resistance and how you can best soften this opposition. Be sure that this study has convinced you of the attitude expressed in number three.

Number six is your next move, followed by numbers eight and ten. This is a very critical stage in selling the improvement you must make. To properly apply effective management techniques, jobs are essential—and improved methods and greater productivity make jobs. So, with considered management judgment, you'll want to use hints numbers one, two, and five. You should then be ready to couple four and nine together in moving on to a successful conclusion of the job improvement you must make. Number eleven must never even be considered because it destroys teamwork, will return to haunt you, and holds the seeds which can ruin your entire career.

How to Use Wages Knowledgeably

There are some things which you as an individual manager are not going to be able to change—at least not in the immediate future. Among these are some significant features which apply to all nonagricultural industry, such as: (1) wage payments, on the average, representing approximately three-fourths of all costs; (2) an average annual increase in wages from 1949 to 1965 of 5 per cent; (3) an average annual gain in productivity of slightly more than 3 per cent for this same period; (4) an average annual increase in the Consumer's Price Index (cost of living) of 2 per cent for this same period; (5) labor unions exercising monopoly power to increase the cost of production.

In meeting these handicaps, effective management provides answers if you recognize the difficulties but accept them as a challenge to be overcome.

Joel Scarter was a successful home builder in a large midwest city. His pattern of operation was to employ small contractors who were specialists in foundations, brickwork, carpentry, electrical installation, plumbing, and all phases of building. This method promoted efficiency and quality work, but local manufacturers with rising wage scales began hiring away the contractors' better workmen.

Joel rightly judged the long-term effects of this development and began to diversify into the marketing of real estate. In this new venture, he used the same decentralized methods which had proved successful in his building business. Thus, as it became increasingly difficult to profitably operate as a builder, Scarter expanded his selling portion of the total business.

On your job you'll find these suggestions helpful: (1) delegate to subordinates substantial and meaningful performance targets; (2) increase the challenge of the employees' work by making it evident that you expect superior results; (3) insure that outstanding accomplishments are adequately rewarded; (4) build loyalties among subordinates with fair treatment; (5) keep alert to wage trends and make sure that your own payment to employees is as good or better than those at competitive, comparable jobs; (6) be flexible and alert, always ready to make changes as appropriate if wage rates force costs up unduly; (7) figure out ways to get returns equal to your increased costs; (8) devise more efficient production methods; (9) install more and better machines; (10) possibly reduce your labor force; (11) improve your distribution and add to your sales.

In essence, what tough going makes you do is manage better. As you succeed in approaching this objective, you create more jobs, at higher wages, with greater output. This enables more people to buy goods at prices which larger numbers of consumers can afford to pay.

Do Your Best to Help Your Company Succeed

You can stimulate new jobs by never missing an opportunity to operate more efficiently on your job.

In the milling department of a large rubber goods manufacturing plant Mike Tohile, the supervisor, was assigned to complete the milling of a rubber-based plasticator. The manager was given specifications which set forth a 20-minute milling time on hot steel rolls set at .003 gauge, followed by straining through a .003 screen, and then remilling at .005 on cold rolls.

It was left to Mike's judgment as to whether he should modify the piecework rate for this job or just pay daywork which, under these conditions, normally equaled average hourly earning. Before making a decision on the wage payment to use, the manager consulted with the five operators affected.

Mike explained that this was a super-quality job. There could not be the slightest deviation from the instructions. He admitted that he wasn't sure what, if anything, would come from their efforts, but their big boss and the chief laboratory superintendent had an air of suppressed excitement when he had been given the job. The manager said, "This could mean a lot to all of us, but not if you just try to make money." Mike then suggested an adjusted piecework rate so that their wages would exceed average hourly earnings as they processed the material, but he emphasized that they must stick right to the gauges, screen sizes, and heat of mill rolls. He cautioned, "When anything doesn't look right to you, call me right away."

With these instructions, the material was started, and you may be sure that it was treated like a newborn baby. It was some time later that Mike was informed that this material was a new sealant compound for swimming pools. After thorough testing, it proved so easy to use, so cheap compared with anything previously developed, and provided such a lasting coating that there was a nationwide demand for the plastic. Because of this new market, an entire new plant was built, and Mike Tohile was promoted to superintendent in charge of manufacturing.

Many new jobs resulted because Mike as a good manager: (1) could, himself, take and carry out orders, (2) made his subordinates active participants in the work they were doing, (3) showed confidence in the workmen's honesty and performance ability, (4) exhibited leadership courage in assigning the work to be done, and (5) used good judgment in evaluating the problem situation as he determined the best way to proceed and meet the difficulties. All these are good tips which you can use in more effectively directing the employees reporting to you.

Many good managers are entitled to a strong measure of the credit for the average annual 920,000 net increase in civilian jobs between 1949 and 1966. By using effective management techniques, you will become one of the sincere, hard-working managers who constantly strive and plan to get better results for their companies— and thus achieve an even better record for creating new jobs.

SUMMARY

1. Select subordinates carefully.

2. Update your people-understanding.

3. Use the magic duo:
    (a) Efficient production.
    (b) Encouraging buyers.

4. Follow the market's road map.

5. Use communication skills to put through improvements.

6. Use wage rates knowledgeably.

7. Improve old products and create new ones.

[1] Gilbert Burck, "The Auspicious Rise of the Soviet Consumer," *Fortune* (August, 1966), p. 132.

[2] Burck, "Rise of Soviet Consumer," pp. 132-33.

[3] *Wall Street Journal* (Dallas), March 30, 1967. John Gray: "Notable & Quotable."

[4] Daniel R. Fusfeld, "The Manpower Revolution," *Michigan Business Review*, XVIII, No. 4 (July, 1966), pp. 13, 16.

7

How to Make the Best Use of Supply, Demand, and Price

Remember that a requirement for success in your job as a professional manager is to let people know that you are "out front" in your work, as a leader must be. You can do this by performing your present job assignment in a way which "shows off" your skills, talents, and abilities. As you carve out a place for yourself in the company for which you work, let your superior know how good you are by doing your present job better than it has been done before.

Among the things that will help you to be a standout manager are an understanding of and the know-how to apply *demand, supply,* and *price.* These three inseparable essentials are necessary if you become a get-attention manager. To appreciate their relationship to each other, think of three oranges in a bowl, each one resting against the other, and labeled individually "Demand," "Supply," and "Price." If you move one, the other two must also move.

An understanding of why this is the normal action pattern of this shifty trio will help you show others that you know the score as you stay on top of your job as a going-places manager.

How the Market Tells What You Can Do

One of the men responsible for the American economic miracle was Henry Ford, who organized his company in 1903. This was before the days of market surveys; and Ford decided in the latter part of the first decade of this century "that Americans would not buy a new automobile every year and that a cheap, simple, sturdy machine—a 'universal car'—was the answer. In 1909 he announced his Model T, a standardized product with the same chassis for all and available 'in any color so long as it was black.'" [1]

To demonstrate a principle which will help you understand what your market tells you, let's make an assumption. At some time in the 18-year period of the Model T's popularity Henry Ford found that at a price of $400 he could pay his total costs, earn a reasonable profit, and sell exactly 300,000 vehicles.

This would be an unusual commercial situation, termed by economists "equilibrium." The shifty trio—demand, supply, and price—are in harmony with each other. The most interesting fact about this "in-balance" condition is that it exists for only a fleeting period. Under the workings of our market economy, equal weighing of the slippery three can only be temporary because of the effects of one or all of these forces which immediately start to work.

First, Mr. Ford was not satisfied with his stationary profit level, so he took one or more of these actions: (a) made more automobiles and kept the $400 price, (b) raised the price of the Model T's, (c) reduced the price and hoped for a greater volume to offset the lower price.

Second, the purchasers can and do refrain from buying automobiles because: (a) men lose their jobs or general economic conditions become depressed; (b) numerous buyers may decide that their wives, girl friends, or children don't need an automobile; (c) wives, girl friends, and/or children may decide they would like a power boat better than a Model T.

Third, the profits invited competitors into the producing and selling of automobiles. These newcomers can and do: (a) reduce costs and offer the buyers a better price, (b) build a more attractive automobile such as General Motors did with Chevrolet in 1927 when Ford countered with the Model A, (c) develop a more effective advertising campaign.

On your job you are selling a service; and, whether you fully recognize it or not, your boss looks at you with dollar signs in his eyes. He asks himself what you contribute that makes him look good, and how well you meet that test determines your get-ahead job power.

Be smart enough to see that your market is repeatedly telling you loudly and clearly that you are a buyer, seller, and receiver of directional services. As an individual manager, you must meet the demands of the market as Henry Ford did with his Model T and, later, with his Model A.

How to Do What the Market Says

Hal Gregg, sales manager for the Chicago-based Stone Container Corp., was rated by his company as a "comer" among their executives. He recently pointed out: "I didn't hold a gun to their heads, but I let them know I was interested in moving up and I thought I was in line for a manager's job." He further remarked, "I always tried to do something extra for the customer. I'd offer to help him with his design problems, with his testing, whatever he wanted. A lot of guys try to get by mainly on personality. Hell, if you get a sale that way a guy with a bigger smile will come along and take it away." [2]

Hal's views are in accord with the accepted functioning of the shifty trio: (1) More buyers are attracted when they get more for their money. (2) As successes come about, more favorable attention comes your way. (3) When you get more customers, your services are worth more.

You have to tailor your management actions to fit the requirements of your specific market, but these principles will help you use the magic three to your advantage:

1. Build yourself a right mental posture. Determine what constitutes demand, supply, and price in your job.

2. Understand the rules and regulate your practices to avoid playing make believe in a world of reality.

3. Be equal to the task. Size up the demands, be aware of competition, and adjust your thinking to meet the costs.

4. Have the "want-to" urge. You can't get the relaxed "will-not-be-beaten" approach of a true professional without a consuming desire to be a front runner.

Remember that one of the primary questions which the market continually asks the ambitious manager is, "How can you do your job more efficiently?"

How to Follow the Demand Road Map

Efficiency of production and its cost are key factors in managing to make the best use of supply, demand, and price. But you must not overlook what your customer continually tells you. The value of this barometer is emphasized by this recently published information: "Prominent Soviet economists have come to realize . . . that their price system doesn't tell them what they need to know. It just doesn't measure value consistently. They are also beginning to recognize that an unrigged, flexible, competitive price system is one of the most sensitive information systems known to man.

"The price system in the West, of course, is only partly free. It is hamstrung by special interests, oligopoly, government controls, and so on. . . . But it works. It automatically puts the values of liter-ally billions of things into fairly consistent and harmonious relation-ships. It automatically offsets shortages, anticipates gluts, rewards quality, foresees needs." [3]

So, it is up to you to gain a better understanding of demand, supply, and price. It can help you evaluate and exercise more re-fined judgments in making decisions about the size of not only the production crew you need, but also the articles you should produce and the quality and number of employees you should strive to effi-ciently use.

You as a successful manager must also remember that economic trouble arises when too many dollars start chasing too few goods. Prices rise and invite competitors; and, if these newcomers turn out to be good producers, they will take your business and leave you without a market. However, this emphasis on supply is not in-tended to minimize the importance of customers. Without buyers, you're without income; and the essential trio readjusts automatically to meet any new or changed situation.

Be Ready for Changes in Your Market

When you appreciate and act upon the changed trends which have developed fairly recently and are continuing, then you'll be doing a better management job. Some of these prevailing tenden-cies are: (1) Soon one-half of the population of the United States will be 25 years of age or less. We can only speculate on the full import of this age revolution. For instance, future managers will probably carry heavier responsibilities at an earlier age; you'll have to time your direction to more radical ideas; you'll have to adjust your thoughts on delegation to meet "the-young-man-in-a-hurry" concept; the older man may find his experience and talents in greater demand; and you'll have to take a closer look at what may be your best motivators. As an example, security could decline on the scale of wants. (2) With tremendous increase in real per capita disposable personal income, the customers you deal with have de-veloped a different outlook from the buyers of a generation ago. Working hours are shorter, vacations longer, and outside interests have increased. Everybody has a favorite sport, hobby, charity, or activity which puts on the pressure for less time at work. All this means that more things must be accomplished in a shorter period of time. Then, too, cultural affairs get more attention. There is a greater interest in history, art, the theater, and writing. Individuals are freer to strive for their own personal expression. (3) The individuals—the people who buy your goods and services—are becoming smarter. This is true in part because of the rapid rise in a broader informational coverage by the mass media: TV, radio, newspapers, magazines. More books are written, published, and sold than ever before. There is a decline in illiteracy and levels of education are increased.

These developments mean that you must be more of a real leader to attract followers. You need to be fully aware that your customers become more convinced every day that they are important. This increased self-appreciation stems from intensive wooing from all sides by people with things to sell. Buyers are learning what constitutes quality, not only in products but in people as well. As separate entities of a total group, individuals are moving forward; and as a manager with out-front ambitions, you must evidence an understanding of the new and added demands of your purchasers.

What You Can Do When Demand Seems Unreasonable

Never discount your boss' intelligence. If he gives you instructions which don't make sense to you, you'd better try for a meeting of the minds.

A large midwestern construction firm won the contract to build a 12-story office building. A bonus was included for early completion and a penalty for failing to meet the completion date.

Lance Sherman, general manager of the firm, in discussing the building details with chief design engineer Frank Norber, pointed out that the top floor beams would require an additional 30° load margin to carry the heating and cooling units. Norber prided himself on his technical competence and resented what he considered Sherman's butting-in on his function. The designer also had visions of sharing substantially in the bonus which the construction com-

pany normally apportioned among key employees for early completion of projects. Frank Norber checked his figures again, allowing
for a normal utility room load, and came out with the same totals;
so he went ahead, finished up, and enclosed the beams without the
extra 30° safety factor.

Some weeks later, when the building was nearing completion well
ahead of schedule, the design engineer congratulated himself because
he had not allowed Lance Sherman's fears to slow him down. Then
Norber learned that an oversized furnace and a new heavy-duty
type air conditioner were to be installed on the top floor so that an
adjoining building as well as the new one could be serviced. Frank
Norber had no choice except to tell Lance that the floor of the
utility room was not strengthened as the general manager had
directed.

Structural changes disrupted the scheduled work, caused a loss of
all the time gained, and the contractor had to pay a few days' penalty time. So, instead of getting a bonus, the construction firm, the
general manager, and the chief design engineer all received a black
eye.

When you are confronted on your job with a situation such as
Frank Norber faced, some lessons you can learn are: (1) Remember
that the man you report to is the person you must satisfy. He is the
demand portion of the demand-supply-price triangle. (2) If what he
tells you to do doesn't make sense, talk with him until you understand why. (3) Don't allow your emotions to distort your judgment.
(4) As a manager, you'll usually be on safer ground to strive for
quality first and let the monetary reward come later. So, as an on-
the-move manager, be sure to know what your job demands are and
meet them in an honest, intelligent fashion.

How to Avoid Killer Costs

To advertise your on-the-job know-how, you must keep reminding
yourself that a compensation to employees in our economy averages
well over 70 per cent of the cost of all products and services. Of
course, to really be a self-promoter you must take action to control
this major cost item. You must use manpower more effectively. You

can't afford to have your operation either under- or overmanned. Instead, you should strive to make full use of what economists call the *marginal output of labor,* which means added output resulting from employment of extra workmen.

Everett Dark, an energetic young man and the operator of a small cushion-making plant for quality furniture, was notified by his two principal customers that his contract with them would be terminated in 60 days. Thus the demand leg of the key trio received a serious blow. In a survey of other possible markets, Dark found a definite trend among larger furniture makers to integrate cushion manufacturing within their own operations as an expected cost-reducing action.

Faced with a vanishing market, Everett Dark considered himself fortunate to be offered the exclusive rights to make a kapok-stuffed personality doll. As an experienced manufacturing manager he realized that his labor cost could either make or break this new operation; so he carefully studied how he might find the most efficient number of workmen to employ. With no increase or decrease in his floor space, machines, or other capital equipment, Everett found that with either four or five workmen the average production per man was 880 dolls; however, since five returned a higher total, this was the most efficient number for the available facilities.

While the total increased with the hiring of each additional man through number nine, after the fifth employee the average output per man decreased because of the limitation of machines, equipment, and floor space. When the eleventh man was added, he got in the way of the other employees and the total output went down.

Faced with a similar situation and trying to control your most expensive cost, what's your best action? You could:

1. Cut your crew to the optimum number costwise.

2. Make further capital investments in tools, machines, equipment, and plant facilities.

3. Add another income product line, such as pillows for the dolls, utilizing the same sewing machines and other facilities and scheduling the added people to work part of their time on the pillows.

4. Operate your plant 24 hours per day.

However, Dark realized he must consider his total costs in relation to manpower, his market, and available additional labor and capital before concluding what should be done. The manager found that, even though marginal output per man declined with the fifth workman and average output declined with the sixth employee, still, when the fixed cost was considered, total average costs were lower when the seventh man was hired. The increase of employees beyond this point then caused average costs to rise. To correctly apply effective management techniques, you must always make the best use of the money you spend to meet the costs which can make or break your success on the job—your manpower costs. This is why it is aptly termed "killer costs" and is one of your most difficult to determine. So, when you are determining the right number of people for an operation, be sure to include all costs in your calculation.

How to Make Prices Work for You

Ransom E. Olds, a pioneer manufacturer of automobiles, first "turned out a complicated car with a pneumatic clutch, cushion tires, and electric starter. Not only was it too far ahead of its day, but it was too expensive, costing $1,250. After one year, Olds began in 1901 to produce a $650 Oldsmobile on a mass basis, buying the parts in quantity, and assembling them on an embryonic assembly line. ... With his improved processes, Olds was turning out 4,000 cars a year by 1904." [4]

Let's analyze some of the price lessons which Olds learned from his first manufacturing experience. By cutting the price approximately in half, he gained these advantages: (1) caused less buyer resistance; (2) tended to discourage too swift competition; (3) the higher volume enabled him to turn over his inventory much faster; (4) enabled him to determine a continuing demand for his car, thus permitting him to establish a more realistic production schedule; (5) this move tended to build goodwill with his customers, encouraging future business.

It is unlikely that you will be given exactly the same kind of an opportunity to make prices work for you that Olds experienced.

However, there are several valuable pointers for you here. For instance, you must be:

1. A forward-looking manager. Keep abreast of the news so you can better judge what's ahead, even though you may not be in a position to introduce a changed product when the market seems right. You can make yourself more valuable to your organization by correctly estimating coming price changes; by anticipating a shortage of skilled help; by accurately gauging a surplus or shortage of important materials that you need on your job; by a better evaluation of the proposals made by subordinates reporting to you.

2. Trained to recognize a good thing when you see it. Remember you'll profit most if you get to the market first with a product others want to buy. This might be a new and better machine, a more efficient way of operating, a reorganization of the work force, or some improvement in the materials used.

3. Thoroughly familiar with all the values to be gained by implementing any proposal that you are trying to sell. To gain acceptance, remember to emphasize any of these benefits: cut costs, improve quality, increase production, make the job safer, build better employee morale, help train and attract superior employees.

4. Willing to express an opinion which you feel has merit. You'll not win every time, but you must keep trying.

Some Helps in Correctly Gauging Your Volume

Decentralization is a popularly voiced objective of top administrative managers. Such an attitude is based upon the sound premise that subsidiaries, divisions, regions, districts, plants, even departments within a plant, will be more profitable if the manager in charge has complete authority, responsibility, and accountability.

In actual practice, however, such complete freedom to call the shots is never exercised. The facts of corporate life make it necessary to standardize such things as: bookkeeping methods, capital borrowing, plant expansion, and maintenance; the wording of union contracts in collective bargaining negotiations; combined purchasing and corporatewide sales; and centralized research and development.

Even where these restrictions are the tightest, a manager with outfront ambitions still has plenty of room to demonstrate his get-results capability. Supply or volume is a place where this stands out sharp and clear. Here again, however, you must consider price and demand as well as the time factor. You must ask yourself, "Is my product an unusual one such as: (1) unsold tickets held by a theater broker on the last night of a show? (2) a passing, short-lived fad item like hula hoops? (3) repeatedly used home appliances, houses, or buildings?" In each of these three situations, demand, supply, and price will differ.

Some other types of demand for your product which will have an effect upon your volume are: (1) a market which can be supplied from inventory or current output, (2) customers who can be satisfied without any additions to fixed capital, and (3) buyers whose demands require that you make additions to fixed assets or resources to supply their needs.

When you have made some judgments on your *supply* market factors and cranked into your estimating the other two members of the shifty trio, *price* and *demand,* you can more accurately determine the volume you should strive to produce.

SUMMARY

1. Keep out front.
2. Allow your market to tell you what to do.
3. Meet the requirements of supply, demand, and price.
4. Remember that employee costs can make or break your operations.
5. Keep prices working for you.
6. Watch for special volume indicators.

[1] Clark Spence, *The Sinews of American Capitalism* (Hill & Wang, 1964), p. 164.

[2] *Wall Street Journal* (Dallas), March 28, 1967, p. 19. Frederick C. Klein: "You're the Boss."

[3] Gilbert Burck, "The Toughest Management Job in the World," *Fortune* (July 1, 1966), pp. 74-77.

[4] Herman E. Krooss, *American Economic Development* (Englewood Cliffs, N. J.: Prentice-Hall, Inc., © 1955), pp. 359-360.

8

How to Be
Wisely Competitive

To do your job really well, it must be very important to you. You must have a tremendous desire to succeed. Remember that no manager suddenly rises to great heights under pressure. You must know the road by having prepared yourself to meet the test.

For superior management teamwork, as a leader you must concentrate on your own personal assignment and carry it out to the best of your ability. You can't afford to stand by and speculate on how well your associates are doing.

It is only under intense competition that you can tell how really good you are. Competition is not merely for the purpose of beating the other fellow; rather, its greatest contribution is to develop your own best performance.

However, as you pursue the path of controlled aggressiveness, be alert to some of the hazards along the way.

How to Gain Some Running Room

"Top management at Bell & Howell's Business Equipment Group has called supervisors together for a series of meetings to listen to their problems and to ask them for possible solutions." One of their recommendations:

"Employee turnover: Many employees who feel qualified for better jobs pack up and quit when they are bypassed in favor of new employees. . . . (Solution:) Set up a companywide talent pool to identify employees who are ready for promotion." [1]

The best utilization of manpower is a common problem in many large business organizations, and the action recommended by the Bell & Howell supervisors can help you to better allocate skilled manpower. However, with the best placement of people there is frequently a hidden efficiency loss—that can be equally costly—which you need to keep on the alert to avoid. Such a waste occurs when a superior employee is promoted and then is so handicapped by an unimaginative manager that he drifts into the get-by rut.

In a large midwestern manufacturing organization, Howard Franks was a first-level engineering supervisor. He was 30 years of age and had been with the company six years. His immediate superior was a manager named Kenneth Herley who was 35 years old and had 11 years of service.

Howard Franks liked his work, used every opportunity for personal development, took his job seriously, worked hard, and welcomed the helpful guidance of Kenneth Herley. He looked forward with confidence to a gradually improving future. This even tenor of events was interrupted when Herley was transferred to another division and his subordinate was advanced to his job. In the new position,

Howard reported to an older manager, in his late forties, named Will Browning.

Howard Franks' advancement was merited, and the promoted manager was enthusiastic and rightly proud of his performance which had permitted this step up. Howard bragged, "I'll do great things. I'm just beginning to get the breaks." Soon the newly advanced manager's ardor began to cool. He made such remarks about his boss as, "His instructions are never clear; and when something goes wrong, it's always my fault. You gotta go by the book. I can't sell him an idea for job improvement. When I do get something started that looks as if it will turn out to have some importance, he turns kibitzer and claims it."

What do you consider some good management relationship principles that Will Browning should have used? Check the statements on the following list that you feel could have helped in getting better results.

1. Howard Franks was too proud of himself. He should have been slowed down.

2. It is usually good practice to give vague instructions to subordinates.

3. Deliberately making an understudy feel inferior is a way to encourage more and better work.

4. Always follow methods you know are in accord with past practices.

5. Subordinates should not be permitted to have too many success experiences.

6. Most people respond with personal self-starter drive and initiative when they are closely supervised.

7. A manager should not be concerned about whether a subordinate has a feeling that he is on top of his job or not.

8. You'll get better results if you remember that nobody really likes any work assignment.

9. A subordinate with on-the-job experience usually causes you more trouble than one you have guided throughout his complete work life.

10. Make it tough for your subordinate to size you up. This will keep him on his toes.

You may want to reread these ten statements. If they indicate Will Browning's management philosophy, what would you do if you were Howard Franks? (1) Have a serious talk with him? (2) Discuss your problem with Will's superior? (3) Ask for a transfer? (4) Look for a job with another company? (5) Accept the situation and try not to let it bother you?

You have probably determined that, without substantial modification, none of the ten stated principles can be recommended as an aid toward building better relationships. Thus, Howard Franks should talk with his superior in an attempt to reach an understanding which will permit him to grow in his job. If this discussion proves unsatisfactory, Franks can suggest that they talk with Will Browning's boss. Depending upon how this conversation turns out, Howard Franks may have to transfer to another department or change companies because healthy competition, both internal as well as external, is the very lifeblood of effective management.

Your determined devotion to self-accomplishment is an essential spark which you must keep alive and glowing.

How to Earn Respect

There can and must be mutual respect between the manager and the subordinate. But as a realistic manager, don't get too shook up if not all the people reporting to you think you're as fine a fellow as you are convinced they should picture you.

Farley Stokes, a first-level engineering manager in the electronics design section of a large factory in Ohio, was unhappy in his job. He went to Griffith Wales, the department head, with the complaint that his superior, Newell Carter, demanded too many favors from him.

When Griffith asked Newell about this allegation, the accused manager responded, "Why, I'm the friendliest guy in the world. Just last week I offered to get up at 6:00 a.m. and drive Farley Stokes to the airport to catch an early flight. My people continually remark about all the trouble I take to do favors for them."

The department head broke into this recital by asking about Carter's relationships with Stokes. The harassed manager enumerated that he had taken this subordinate into his home scores of times for steaks and went out with him to various social events. Recently he had taken Farley to a headquarter divisional meeting to let him get better acquainted with those who would be helpful to him.

Griffith Wales next asked what Stokes meant about the business of doing favors for him, and Newell Carter quickly responded that this just didn't make sense. Then, after thinking for a few seconds, he did recall that Farley Stokes had made him an attachment for his stereo. In defense of his action, Carter claimed that Stokes liked to do that sort of work and that he did more favors for his subordinate than he received in return. Newell Carter added that sometimes his subordinate did come by and give him a ride to the office, but that wasn't much out of his way.

The department head advised Newell Carter to assist Farley Stokes in finding a satisfactory position in another department. Griffith Wales further suggested that Carter should seriously consider these facts of value to any manager:

1. You are not supposed to win a popularity contest. You can't avoid decisions which favor one subordinate over another; thus, someone is very likely to be unhappy. It is more important that you be right, fair, and impartial than that all the people reporting to you love you.

2. Work for the respect of others; and, if you can earn a little more, that's gravy.

3. Try to give subordinates work they like to do, and let them do it. Working toward an objective permits them to meet a challenge and compete for a purpose. Busy people often forget to personalize what someone else does or doesn't do to or for them.

4. Have regular reviews to spot developing troubles. You can't shut your eyes and have problems go away.

5. Strive for improved communications. Don't hide your personal enthusiasm. Let others know when they are winning. Direct attention to your management know-how by helping those reporting to you beat their own best performance.

6. It is an unhealthy management practice to give and accept favors from subordinates.

Intelligent aggressiveness applied without discrimination is essential to the proper working of effective management techniques. You are being wisely competitive when you practice these safeguards in cultivating right relationships with *all* your associates.

Influence Subordinates with Your Can-Do Philosophy

Douglas McGregor, recognized authority on management education, said: "I thought I could avoid being a 'boss' ... I thought that maybe I could operate so that everyone would like me—that 'good human relations' would eliminate all discord and disagreement.

"I could not have been more wrong. It took a couple of years, but I finally began to realize that a leader cannot avoid the exercise of authority, any more than he can avoid responsibility for what happens to his organization. This notion is not in the least inconsistent with humane, democratic leadership. Good human relations develop out of strength, not out of weakness." [2]

To get the most mileage out of your proper relationships with others requires that you have more than just a smile, a happy greeting, and a jolly good fellow attitude. You have to earn your leadership by problem solving, knowing what to do at the right time, and being willing to make decisions.

You must conduct your direction of others so that they: (1) grasp some reasons why an organized effort is necessary, (2) are given some opportunities to use their capabilities, (3) get encouragement to make personal improvements, (4) have a fair shake in competing for a higher station on the economic ladder, (5) may better understand their own responsibility to the organization of which they are a part, (6) feel, personally, some of the pressures and excitement of our economic society's win-or-lose philosophy.

How You Benefit from Curbs on Competition

In the can't-be-stopped climate in which successful managers work, you need to remember some of the slowdown brakes on unrestrained competition. Responding to the urge of competition, you naturally strive to make judgments and take actions which, if carried to their ultimate conclusion, would give your company a product or service monopoly.

Without enforcement of antitrust rules of fair competition, you would not have the professional opportunities offered by: (1) more than 5 million individually owned businesses now operating in this country for the first time, (2) more effective use of scarce resources, (3) more discriminating buyers, (4) steadily increasing economic growth, (5) a wider range of product choices, (6) the encouragement to operate more efficiently, to use your talents to develop methods, to increase the stream of new and better products and/or services.

These are all advantages of the free market. However, when reference is made to the free market, it is meant only in a relative sense. You should recognize that many deviations exist in a real business situation which restrict competition. The same is true with your job as a manager. Entirely free, wide-open competition would be disastrous. Individualism is desirable, but personal interests must be subservient to what is best for the total organization. Such self-control can rightly be termed disciplined competition.

To practice this builder-upper, you will find Fort Squires' formula helpful in your own management situation. Fort picked his goals early and earned a top 10 per cent grade point in his university graduating class. He was careful to accept a job from a company which stressed early identification and development of future middle and top managers.

Fort attracted attention by working harder than his associates. He realized that it was impossible to overlook an employee who is noticeably eager. The young employee wasn't concerned where his workplace happened to be, whether he was first in line for the coffee break, or if he hit the clock right at quitting time.

The ambitious young comer took every opportunity to get acquainted with people; talk with them about their work, ideas, hobbies; listen to whatever they wanted to say. He read not only the newspaper but also business magazines and good books (not necessarily business-oriented). At every opportunity, Fort studied what other employees were doing and how they handled their jobs. The young man joined a political party, became a precinct committee-man, and learned from this activity that you must work hard to persuade people that your ideas are good in a private nonstructured organization. Fort Squires found this was helpful on-the-job self-discipline.

Such a straightforward and energetic competitor, of course, was soon quietly identified as a future manager.

Thus, if you want to be on your way, as Fort found himself, toward a demanding and rewarding position in management, these are some of the things you must do:

1. Get all the education you possibly can—specialized, if this is important to you—but throw in some broadening outside reading and associations.

2. Choose your company carefully; even wait, if you can't convince yourself which is the right one to select.

3. When you join up, give it all you've got. More and more employment specialists complain that the young prospective employee is primarily interested in fringe benefits, vacations, pensions, time off, health and accident insurances, and security. This gives you a wide-open field to be an individualist by showing yourself to be first and foremost a producer, the rare one who is not interested in "something for nothing."

4. Let everybody and every experience teach you. Have an open mind, ready to absorb the significance of events around you.

5. Avoid preconceptions which may be misleading. Examine happenings for the minuses as well as the pluses; look for a fresh meaning, a new viewpoint.

These are some of the ways you can use disciplined competition for your own and your company's benefit, as you are alert to the advantages which stem from the use of effective management techniques.

How to Beat Unfair Restrictions

To be wisely competitive, you need to know how to deal with limitations on your ability to compete. As a first step, you must distinguish between right and wrong tactics before you can handle this job requirement.

Let's check a few examples which you would identify as unfair competition. Place a "u" after those you consider to be in this category.

1. In April 1967 the U. S. Supreme Court upheld the right of carpenters *not* to install precut doors.   _____

2. When the police enforce an ordinance which prohibits door-to-door selling.   _____

3. When State laws require that nationally branded products cannot be sold below an established minimum price.   _____

4. A union-shop provision requiring membership in a union is written in a labor union agreement.   _____

5. Federal-government-legislated minimum wage levels.   _____

6. Farm subsidy payments for limiting production.   _____

7. Tariffs on manufactured goods which protect and reward inefficiency.   _____

8. Government-operated printing plants.   _____

9. Government-operated public utilities such as electric power plants, water service, and transportation.   _____

10. A few large corporations dominating an industry such as the manufacture of automobiles.   _____

11. Being employed by a company which continually loses money.   _____

12. Being employed in a company which doesn't believe in any research, advanced planning, or special development efforts.   _____

As an alert manager you can handle unethical practices; you can avoid becoming involved. However, the checklist does pose some real management problems as you strive to remain competitive:

1—This is an artificial restriction against using the most efficient manufacturing and building methods. To remain wisely competitive, you must find a way to make use of the latest technological advances. A practical course may be to negotiate this right into the union contract. Another alternative is to find an offsetting improvement.

2 and 3—These are similar handicaps to the sale of products and services—enforced by law designed to protect the market for local merchants. There is some legal opinion that these so-called fair trade laws are illegal. To overcome this hurdle, you might brand your own products, sell through a local distributor, or through a mail order catalog. It might even work to get the law changed to encourage competition.

4—Required membership in a labor union can cripple your ability to compete as a professional. Fortunately unions do not extend to management employees in most businesses and industries. However, strong union pressure, tending toward monopoly, can force you to manage better as a way to compensate for excessive labor costs.

5—Government-legislated minimum wages encourage managers to turn to machines as a replacement for the lowest skilled employees. You will search for means to automate your operations in direct relationship to the increased cost of labor.

6 and 7—These are each artificial interruptions to normal competitive forces. Supply, demand, and cost should, to the extent that other nations will cooperate, be allowed to operate freely, worldwide.

8 and 9—When the government sets up shop in your business, you as a private operator are handicapped in the competition for the customer's dollar.

10—This is possibly the only statement that you should not mark as unfair. In the present economy, a few big companies compete more vigorously than many small ones because they have more resources. You should also not overlook the fact that competition exists within the large companies, one division with another.

11 and 12—Management has a first responsibility to earn a profit for the company they direct. Lack of look-ahead planning, research, and development is evidence of a dying company and should be your warning to look for another job.

Even though some of these barriers to competition may seem to be largely outside your control as an out-front manager, you should, at a minimum, take these actions: (1) Don't relax and become complacent in the luxury of *any* shelter from the pressures of competition. (2) Examine your possible alternatives to determine what course you might follow if full competition should be restored. (3) Explore the gains you might obtain from a return to open competition.

Some Ways to Retain Your Get-Ahead Spirit

Competition in all phases of business is increasing and will continue to grow, so don't allow your spirit of forward-looking aggressiveness to become depressed.

The thing that is important to you determines what you'll do. The famous former coach of the phenomenally successful University of Oklahoma football team, Bud Wilkinson, relates a story which illustrates this fact. Mr. Wilkinson tells of the year in which Texas A & M was completing a championship season with the final game against Arkansas, which A & M was picked to win by four touchdowns.

The Texas A & M team was coached by Paul (Bear) Bryant, noted as a stern disciplinarian. The quarterback was a young fellow named Osborne, a talented football player in all these superior performance abilities: intelligent; clever ball handler; good kicker, passer, and defensive man. His only weakness was that he wasn't noted as a fast runner.

It was a difficult day for the A & M team; and, with less than two minutes left to play, with the score 7 to 0 in their favor, they had the ball on their own five-yard line, first down. The 50,000 people in the stands, all the members of the opposing team, and most of his own team expected Osborne to "run out the clock" with safe, into-the-line plays. Instead, the quarterback decided to throw a pass into the flat, score a touchdown, and thus in part achieve a better portion of the victory they were supposed to score.

An alert Arkansas back intercepted the pass and started down the sideline with no one between him and the goal. Osborne streaked across the field with lightning speed, which startled everyone, and forced the Arkansas ballcarrier out of bounds on the three-yard line. The Texas A & M team had a strong defense which held until the end of the game, coming out the winner 7 to 0.

As the team left the field, a disappointed Arkansas assistant coach said to one of his counterparts on the A & M team, "We'll never believe you again. You've been saying all year that Osborne couldn't run." The A & M coach replied, "While your back was running for a touchdown—you know Bear Bryant—Osborne was running for his life."

Coach Wilkinson says that he used to question his squad each year, "How good do you really want to be? I can help you, but I can't make you any better than you really want to be."

In the production planning department of a large metal products assembly plant, a young, newly appointed manager, Charles Finley, reported to Dorth Williams, a supervisor of many years' job experience.

Finley had a good formal education with about one year of employment in a related department, and he had finished an orientation course in his company's management training program. He tackled his first assignment with evident enthusiasm. Right away he decided that the filing system was all wrong—too much duplication of work. This young go-getter decided that the answer was to set up a specialist group to do nothing but filing.

When Charles Finley suggested his idea to his boss, the older manager quickly replied, "Oh, we tried that years ago. It didn't work." The new supervisor thought, "That's not the way to handle a man with an idea. I'll have to try to benefit from that experience."

Later, in talking with Clifton Ray, a senior planner, he asked, "Do you recall an experiment some time back when a crew of specialists were assigned to filing, and what happened?" The old-timer replied, "I'm not sure they had a fair chance, for before the kinks could be worked out, Dorth Williams decided that planners could best develop themselves by digging out the complete details independently." Then the senior employee continued, "I've had an idea for a long time that all the needed information could be put on an IBM run, entirely eliminating the files." This caused Charles Finley to ask himself how each planner could get the information he must have. What about the boss' idea of developing planners?

The young manager checked the IBM section and was assured by these experts that they could handle part, if not all, of the filed information. The section supervisor also told him that as many copies of the listing as needed could be made with no difficulty. Finley gave his problem some further thought, checked some additional angles, and was ready for a repeat performance with his superior.

After trying to pick a favorable time, the ambitious manager still found his superior obviously hostile when he started to discuss the filing practices of the department. Dorth Williams growled, "You're wasting your time. You've got to realize that we are just in a part of the business in which some overlap and repeated checking is necessary to get the job done. If you want to get ahead on your job, just crack the whip over those loafers reporting to you." Finley, however, didn't quit, but said, "They are doing well and I'll keep an eye on them, but I also want to try some new angles with the IBM fellows."

His superior sighed, "You're certainly persistent. I suppose if it doesn't interfere with your regular work that you might try some experiments. However, remember I want those fellows to stay on schedule."

To help you retain your get-ahead spirit, there are several significant principles you should remember and apply:

1. Charles Finley found the way to keep his assignment interesting. By looking for possible improvements, he kept a fresh challenge always ahead and thus avoided the deadening routine of doing things in the same way over and over.

2. Once the new manager seized upon what he thought was a good idea, he didn't quit. You're paid to use judgment; and if you don't risk failure now and then, your company will not get full value from your abilities and skills.

3. Finley exhibited the qualities of a good competitor. He's an individualist with sufficient self-assurance to earn the respect of even a hostile superior.

4. This coming manager was also a realist. He accepted the facts of a hierarchical authority within the framework of a business organization. His persistence in getting his immediate superior's approval can supply a valuable tip to you.

5. Finley got a double return by bringing his subordinate into the problem. He was able to uncover leads to the solution of his prob-

lem, and he deposited some encouragement money in the bank which will pay interest toward the solution of future difficulties. This will also build stronger subordinates for the future.

On your present assignment, you can directly benefit from being wisely competitive. Stay alert for chances to show you have good ideas and develop enough fortitude to carry them through to a successful conclusion.

How to Pick and Use Challenging Opportunities

Your advancement can be retarded, ambitions frustrated, and even your career wrecked if you fail to heed the signs which flash warning lights, alerting you about how you can better advertise your capabilities.

In the subassembly shop of a midwestern manufacturing plant, Phil Torrey and Grant Jenkins, each first-level managers in their early thirties with approximately equal years of service, were being compared for promotion to the job of department head. A direct evaluation was made easier because both were supervising crews in the same department.

Phil Torrey was an excellent technician; he knew the machinery and how much an average workman should do in a standard shift. He understood company policies and generally was respected by the people reporting to him. Torrey had a temper which flared up and caused him to bawl out a subordinate occasionally, but, offsetting this, he tended to shoulder everyone's problem.

Because he was a very sensitive personality, Phil Torrey keenly felt the need for self-improvement. He took advantage of all the study courses offered by the company and learned as much as time permitted by visiting other factory operations. However, he shied away from the part of the training program that permitted temporary assignments in other departments.

Phil Torrey displayed a valuable ability in that he seldom missed in determining when a man could handle a job. After he had made his judgment and assigned the job, he allowed his subordinate to make the decisions and carry out his work. Frequently Phil checked himself by asking, "What am I doing and why am I doing it?" It was his policy to farm out to his understudies: (1) the things they could do best, (2) assignments that would help them grow, and (3) jobs that were time-consuming and interfered with his own thinking and planning time.

Grant Jenkins was a cold, unemotional type who gave the impression that he wasn't going out of his way to help anyone unless it was clearly an advantage to the job operation. All requests for employment were referred to the employment department. His self-control kept him from ever openly expressing anger.

Jenkins had a high regard for his own personal qualities. To him, formal classroom studies were a waste of time; on-the-job experience was the payoff. He liked the idea of displaying his competence in another department; new problems and challenges were his meat.

It was Grant Jenkins' practice to delegate only the most minor and routine duties to his subordinates, paying little attention to any special talents displayed by employees reporting to him. Grant drove himself continuously to keep abreast of the rapid development in his industry and only with reluctance could be persuaded to take a vacation.

Carson Ferrall was the plant manager who had to determine which of the two candidates was to be promoted. To help him in this judgment, he made this listing:

Torrey

Strengths:

1. Technical knowledge of machinery, people, and their productive capabilities.

2. Understanding of company policies, plus the earned respect of the people reporting to him.

3. Willingness to help others.

4. Studying of formal courses and other departments for self-improvement.

5. Good judgment of the capabilities of people.

6. Belief in real delegation: allows his subordinates to use their ingenuity and special abilities.

7. Uses a formula for checking himself—a method of measuring his management effectiveness.

Weaknesses:

1. Tendency to be too softhearted.
2. Fails to control angry outbursts which generate resistance.
3. Lack of confidence in his management ability to tackle an unfamiliar assignment.

Jenkins

Strengths:

1. Strong central interest in getting the job done.
2. Superior personal self-confidence.
3. Willingness to meet new problems and challenges.
4. Dedicated to being a hard worker at his job.

Weaknesses:

1. Short on human sensitivity.
2. Ignores advantages he could gain from formal education.
3. Alienates some people because of aggressive egotism.
4. Poor delegator.
5. Not smart in handling the brainwork portion of his job.

From this listing, Carson Ferrall reasoned that Phil Torrey displayed the more valuable good qualities, that he was more flexible, and his weaknesses could be more readily corrected. Thus, the boss surmised that in a familiar department Torrey's confidence could more quickly be built up. Ferrall had a long conversation with the manager he had chosen before he promoted him. As a part of this conversation, he warned Phil about being too easy a mark for another's sob story and cautioned him to control his temper.

The boss also had a talk with Grant Jenkins and explained why he had chosen Torrey for the job. Carson Ferrall commended the losing manager on his strong points and made some suggestions about his weaknesses. The payoff for this thoughtful handling of a difficult situation was evident when Jenkins was assigned to a promotional opening in another department within three months.

Phil Torrey met the requirements of his new job in splendid fashion, which convinced the boss that this subordinate, with proper coaching, could advance to even higher levels of responsibility.

Be ready for the opportunities in a competitive challenge by: (1) clearly defining your strengths, (2) putting these advantages to work for you, (3) admitting your weaknesses to yourself, (4) erecting some safeguards against career damage from these shortcomings, and (5) striving to correct your weaknesses as a manager. Such a self-evaluation will pay you dividends.

How to Work Hard Without Damaging Your Personal Success Machinery

Admiral "Bull" Halsey once said, "There are no great men, only great challenges that ordinary men are forced by circumstances to meet." Certainly the opportunity must be present which enables ordinary men to rise to greatness. You either know or will learn from experience that there is no better proving ground for greatness than management in business or industry.

But, remember, the job isn't easy: "Competition and tension are inseparable. Both are healthful. But when they are continued too long or become too intense, physical symptoms may appear. Sleeplessness, fatigue, irritability, and indigestion are some such symptoms." [3]

To be a wise competitor, you've got to be healthy physically and mentally. Aggressiveness is an attribute which you must encourage; but, at the same time, you must keep fit—be ready to meet the challenges which frequently and unexpectedly jolt a manager.

Here are some practical rules which will keep you in the race:

1. Cultivate a philosophy. Many managers let a strong fear of losing handicap their action and thoughts. Such an attitude is unhealthy. It is helpful to remind yourself that in any competition which you are really trying to win, even if you don't come out on top, you have earned some valuable benefits. You've stored up ammunition for future contests; you've sharpened your competitive senses; you've enjoyed the thrill of trying your talents against a worthy opponent.

2. Get regular physical exercise. Make this effort competitive: stretch yourself either against an opponent or your own record. It is only through this kind of exertion that job tensions can be relieved.

3. Develop a pride in being the master of yourself. This can be one of your most difficult challenges, but the payoff is worth the effort.

Many managers who find themselves "under the gun" or who face a "must-perform" situation seek escape in alcohol, sleeping pills, and tranquilizers. Be boss of yourself.

4. Search out the opportunities which are always present in any manager's job to demonstrate creative ingenuity. To get ahead in your profession, you must do better than comparable managers. You're on your way when you get more, better, lower-cost, on-schedule production than your competitor.

Look on your personal success machinery as: a clear mind; healthy body; aggressive attitude; a willingness to take some calculated risks; a free-wheeling, "I-can-handle-this-problem" outward confidence—which stems from past successes and inner self-assurance. Remember, the only way you can keep this equipment well-oiled is to use it competitively.

How to Have the Right Successor
Ready at the Right Time

To serve your own interest, you must help those reporting to you.

(1) Don't allow personal competitiveness to prevent you from bringing along your best subordinate to take your place. (2) You'll get better results by being frank with your understudy. Tell him why you want him to develop himself. Help him decide where he needs strengthening. (3) Be free with your time for this purpose. It's important to you. Avoid being critical and use patience. (4) Check up to evaluate what you are accomplishing after an appropriate time period. Whether you forge ahead or change course, each of you need to know how the plan is progressing.

Fred Hight was a competent, ambitious manager in his mid-thirties. He had worked hard and earned promotions upward through the finance department of a large company. One day while talking with Brent Sidel, a veteran manager from the production section, Hight mentioned that his follow-up man, Max Stalrup, was far below what he ought to be in understanding pricing practices, internal audit methods, and in the use of acceptable methods of directing the people reporting to him.

Brent Sidel expressed immediate concern as he said, "You've got to do something to correct that situation. Why, those are some of the most important functions you handle. And if you don't have a competent follow-up man, you'll not get a chance to step up to a higher position."

The younger man agreed, but asked, "Do you think I should try a new man?" The older manager replied, "I'd try to bring Max up to a satisfactory standard first; later you might want to consider a replacement—but do something right now."

Fred Hight went back to his office, thought about his problem, made some notes, and then called in his subordinate. The superior told Max that he had been doing a good job as evidenced by his position as Hight's understudy. However, the boss added, "You know how rapidly things change in our business, so I want you to be ready to take over my job with a very minimum of delay. This means that you'll have to learn more about my total responsibility. With this in mind, where do you feel you need some help?"

Somewhat to the boss' surprise, Max picked out pricing and internal audit. After some further discussion, the subordinate also agreed that he wasn't as tactful with people at all times as he might be. The two managers concluded that Stalrup would spend 30 days in the pricing section and an equal amount of time in internal audit; he would take an evening course in Human Relations and put some of the principles into practice on the job. At the end of 90 days, Fred and Max got back together for a checkup on what had been accomplished. After reviewing the record, both were astonished at the progress which had come about. Within the next three months, the superior had an opportunity for a substantial promotion which he was able to accept because his understudy was ready to take over his work.

Remember, your boss is always interested in continuity; and, before you can move up, he'll want to know that your job will be adequately filled.

SUMMARY

1. Maintain a strong desire to move up in management.
2. Remember that good managers need some running room.
3. Strive to earn the respect of your associates.
4. Influence subordinates with your competitive philosophy.
5. Learn to benefit from controls on wide-open competition.
6. Recognize and meet unfair restrictions.
7. Take your knockdowns and come back for more.
8. Push your strengths to the forefront.
9. Develop a win philosophy, watch your health, master yourself, practice creative ingenuity.
10. Have an understudy ready to move up.

Notes to Chapter 8

[1] Bruce Trabue, ed., "It's Management's Turn to Listen," *The Manager's Letter* (July 20, 1967), p. 3.

[2] "Leadership and Motivation," *Conference Board Record*, Vol. III, No. 8 (August, 1966), p. 48.

[3] Harry Johnson, M.D., "The Executive Asks the Doctor," *Business Management* (September, 1966), p. 21.

III

**STEP UP TO A MORE RESPONSIBLE
JOB BY STRETCHING YOUR
PERFORMANCE TO MEET
YOUR POTENTIAL**

III

9

How to Get Your
Success-Multiplier
Working

A touch of inspiration will help you hustle up your talents to stretch your reach for the outer perimeters of your potential. It'll make possible accomplishments you thought far beyond your grasp.

In your job as an effective manager, you've got to stretch your own abilities to reach your leadership potential; and providing inspiration is one of the ways you can help others perform so that they produce at higher levels of quality and quantity.

How to See the Big Picture

For most people, there is a strong sense of exhilaration in being part of a group which is going somewhere and doing something worthwhile. It's up to you to help your subordinates see the target toward which you are striving.

Arthur W. Cowles, a vice-president of the Koppers Company, in talking with a selected group of managers said, "There is a bridge in Pittsburgh. It is a graceful bridge arching over the Allegheny River, and those responsible for designing and building it can be justly proud of their work.

"It has, however, a shortcoming that is absolutely fatal for bridges: It doesn't get to the other side.

"Apparently the capable people involved in planning and building this bridge and its approaches were so immersed in their respective, specialized tasks that no one thought to determine whether the necessary steps had been taken to clear the land rights to the north bank. An incredible oversight, of course. But lest we be too harsh in our judgment, let us remember that this mistake, while of dramatic proportions, differs only in degree from the kinds of errors of omission and commission that form a part of our lives in today's specialized, compartmentalized world.

"More often than not in the specialist's world, there is a high order of competence coupled with dedication to the specific task. But what frequently is lacking is the quality that can be characterized only as *total involvement* and surely, if there had been total involvement on someone's part, the elegant bridge that leads to nowhere would have completed its leap across the river." [1]

One of the things which will help you become totally involved in your work is to have an understandable and usable priority list of duties to be accomplished. In setting up such a program, the first step you must take is to examine your problems.

The Mate Company manufactured a cheap, mass-produced grade of household furniture. The plant operated on an around-the-clock basis with a first-level manager directing each of three shifts consisting of crews of from 18 to 20 men. On second, the 2:30 p.m. to 11:00 p.m. work shift, Bert Shram was a young manager who made a special attempt to know the people reporting to him. In general, they were highly experienced, but several were handicapped by personal troubles of various kinds.

Added to Bert's problems was the general agreement that production should be greater on his shift because of less experimental activity and fewer new workmen to train, each of which was considered a handicap on first and third shifts respectively. Thus Bert Shram was under pressure from both the preceding and following shifts.

Bert also recognized that the oak timbers from which his crew fashioned panels, later staining them to the furniture makers' specifications, were too often improperly cured, warped, and overly knotty. The busy manager felt sometimes that his material supplier deliberately saved the worst material to be delivered on second shift.

Other special problems on second shift were an evident reluctance by the repairs manager to keep the equipment in tip-top shape and an assignment to inspect and dispose of substandard furniture.

The variety and complexity of Bert Shram's problems are about the normal difficulties confronting the average manager on his job. In this kind of a job environment where unexpected problems continually arise, a specific priority list is essential if you hope to stay on top of your many-faceted responsibility.

A test and a challenge for you is how well you exercise good judgment in putting first things first. After you accept this formula as a prime requirement, your schedule must not be set in concrete. Allow some flexibility. A helpful guide in assisting you to see the big picture is:

1. List the details you must take care of, such as routine reports, check of possible trouble spots, and a review of down-the-road duties.

2. Personally review each subordinate's performance, satisfying yourself that delegated duties are being handled. Be alert for developing troubles of all types.

3. Make allowances on your priority list for the unexpected. Don't be bogged down in detail when an emergency situation arises.

4. If you are the kind of manager who will get ahead, you must have some "think time" to use in determining how you can do your job better. Make sure you don't spend all your energy putting out fires or getting yourself so busy chopping wood that you fail to take time to sharpen the axe.

To stretch for your potential, take time to sit down with your boss and review your priorities schedule. He'll appreciate your insight into your planned way for making personal interest and enthusiasm pay off. This will also help you stimulate your success-multiplier by determining whether there's a market for what you're selling.

This is an important fact to determine. "Paul Zinkann built a better mousetrap, but nobody beat a path to his door.

"Mr. Zinkann is president of Pioneer Tool & Die Co., Akron, Ohio, which in 1956 built a baitless, odorless, automatic trap that catches mice by the dozens. About the size of an attaché case, the elaborate device lures curious rodents, one at a time, to scurry into a hole, through a trapdoor, along a corridor, and onto a plank that plunges them to their deaths in a water-filled compartment.

"Pioneer built 5,600 of the traps—and lost $63,000 when customers bought only 400, at $29.95 each. The company finally scrapped 5,000 traps. Mr. Zinkann is still trying to sell the remaining 200 for $15 each. 'Our big mistake was that nobody ever found out whether any-one wanted to buy a mousetrap as elaborate as ours for the original high retail price,' he says." [2]

A part of getting a look at your big picture is to determine whether your boss wants to buy the service you're selling at the price he must pay. To practice the total involvement that such a determina-tion requires, some further tips will be helpful.

How to Work in Trouble-Loaded Situations

As a manager you would find it more pleasant to have someone else tell the below-average performer that he will have to be re-placed; the surplus employee that he is due for a layoff; or any subordinate one or more of the innumerable, disagreeable facts of organization life. However much you may like to avoid these painful realities, it can't be done because these unpleasant duties are a part of the job. At best, you can reduce the incidents and temper their severity.

One of the first actions to practice in achieving this goal is to *know where you are going.* The general manager of the Allegheny River bridge in Pittsburgh failed to secure the land rights to the north bank and thus found himself with a fine but useless bridge because it went nowhere. The Pioneer Tool & Die Co. lost money on a fine product because the price was too high. By looking ahead you can decide what is needed to get where you want to go. Select a plan to accomplish the objective you have set, and dodge the foreseeable hazards. *Benefit from experience.* Use care in analyzing the circumstances, the action taken, and the results of your decisions.

Chad Heine was assigned by the plant manager as a department head in charge of production planning and the new business efforts of a large company. Chad inherited a group of key, long-service employees, most of whom he was informed handled their work as if they were just marking time until retirement.

Heine quickly asked some questions and gave some directions which required the members of his crew to give attention to several detailed operating-improvement proposals. These suggested approaches emphasized creativity and some just plain, hard work. The new department manager also set a time limit for reporting results. Some of the reactions from his crew were: excuses that the jobs were too difficult, time was too short, they couldn't get cooperation from other departments. Chad Heine refused to be drawn into these evident, alibi-establishing endeavors. Instead, he just smiled and pointed to the scheduled reporting dates. The crew members surprised themselves when many new, workable ideas were submitted before the final deadline. Chad's boss told the department manager that some of the old-timers who had brought complaints to him about the way they were being treated were now, for the first time in years, showing some signs of enthusiasm for their jobs.

Of course, not all the crew members responded affirmatively to this kind of direction. Some flopped. With these, Chad had some private conversations which resulted in a second chance for a few and transfers and retirements for others. The outstanding significance of the newly appointed manager's actions was that the department started to become more productive. You can do the same when you apply the balance principles learned from your experience to your job problems. These guides can be spelled out: *First:* Determine the similarity and differences between the current problem situation and past happenings. *Second:* Can you use the same action measures that were taken in one of these earlier experiences? *Third:* Have your past results been completely satisfactory? Are there further improvements which would be practical and desirable?

As you work under the pressures of your job responsibilities, here are some further rules to follow:

Maintain control. You're the leader and this means that you can't panic. You must have looked ahead and anticipated some difficulties. Those which arise unexpectedly you must meet squarely as Chad Heine did. In getting his department back into an efficiently functioning unit, he refused to listen to alibi reasons why selected goals could not be reached. By holding firmly to his purpose, Chad supplied the leadership force which brought out the best operators as well as uncovering the failures among his subordinates.

Act on your best judgment. When you reach a conclusion, do something about it. You can't be a leader without action. Department manager Chad Heine demonstrated this in his trouble-loaded assignment. He took the initiative by insisting that employees reporting to him use imagination and hard work, and accomplish the job to be done in a reasonable time.

To flex your potential-reaching muscles and get your success-multiplier working, be as sure as practical of your chosen action course.

Some Ways to Test Your Judgment

It is a maxim that good judgment must be considered one of the important keys to balanced management. On your job as a manager you continually face decisions which test your judgment. Here are some useful principles: *First,* you can cultivate and use reliable sources of information. One of these is a knowledge of general economic facts which are helpful, such as the spending and saving habits of the members of our society. Another is the relationship of all the earning, spending, and profiting elements of our economy. Still another is what it takes to make this roundabout, input-output process continue to function.

Second, you can use the opinions of others. Suppose that you are a second-level manager directed by your boss to reduce the overhead cost on your operation. You have subordinate managers whom you can consult for recommendations. If you maintain the "right" management atmosphere, you can also get help from most workmen. Then, too, it is frequently desirable to discuss such common management problems with other veteran managers, not necessarily in your direct line of organization.

However, you must weigh the facts you acquire. Remember that an important guide must be your informant's reliability.

Third, use your full knowledge. As you gain experience as a manager, you'll realize that questions for decision don't come to you clearly marked "This is important" or "This is not so critical." When you take an action or refrain from acting, it reflects upon your career —either good or bad. When your boss wants results on his cost-reduction order, you must attack this problem right away. When your judgment is required on anything relating to your job, whether it appears to be important or unimportant, be sure to give it your entire attention. If you treat your decision casually and fail to look at all the possible facets, the aftermath will likely come back to haunt you at what you can bet will be the most inappropriate time.

Fourth, back your decision with courage. Many times on your job you must act without any sure knowledge of what people will do or what the final outcome will be.

How to Get Success-Multiplier Benefits in Your Managing

As you reach the position of a true professional in your field, one of the tests you continually face is that of expanding your influence. Identifying human urges supplies a key to effective management techniques. To increase your powers, you must not only know but adapt and direct these urges to productive purposes.

The first of these multipliers which the other person has that you need to get going for you is *the desire to be somebody.* You'll benefit by distinguishing your followers as individuals.

A second multiplier is *to become active in a worthwhile cause.* The people you lead must feel they know where they are going and that what they are striving for is a goal worth attaining.

A third multiplier is *to gain a feeling of belonging.* Your subordinates need a sense of security and participation in their jobs.

See how many of these multipliers you can correctly identify. Mark 1, 2, or 3 after each to indicate your choice of one of the human drives just discussed:

1. The manager told his crew, "This is the first stage of the rocket which will take our astronauts to the moon, so we'll need extra careful workmanship." _____

2. The first-shift union steward said, "You could be president of our union in a couple of years. People already look to you for guidance." _____

3. The first-shift manager told his superior, "I'm proud of this crew. You can't beat them." _____

4. "Jim, you're my first choice for boss of that critical heat-treat job if you'll get your college degree." _____

5. "Ralph, I hope you never decide to go over to our competitor. We'll be lost without you." _____

6. "Boys, it's up to our department to keep the company from losing a chunk of money this month." _____

7. "Who's going down to give some blood for those fellows who got burned in the electric plant fire?" _____

8. "Every man in the department is making at least 10 per cent over his quota. How about you?" _____

9. "The crew on the flight line is waiting for this assembly. You know that airplane delivers today." _____

10. "Charlie, I wish I had your knack of finding the troubles in those electric motors." _____

11. "That assembly plant in Kansas City will know some real operators are on the job here when they get these parts—and this far ahead of schedule, too." _____

12. "Joe, you haven't been late or absent for a whole year." _____

You may have to ponder each of these 12 to match the statement with the proper multiplier. It may be, too, that you'll want to place more than one figure after some. This is fine because the real value to you is to adapt these multipliers in your management to secure your on-the-job benefits.

To check our judgment of the multipliers, I marked as number one: 2, 4, 8, 11, and 12; number two: 1, 6, 7, and 9; number three: 3, 5, 10, and 9.

A tip for you in getting the success-multiplier working for you is to strive for a breakthrough—*a first*. Then, whether it's an individual or your entire crew, keep the ball rolling. Nothing succeeds like success.

To attract the benefits of these multipliers, keep them in the forefront of your thinking as you: (1) Direct all your attention to the problem confronting you. (2) Never give up, no matter how black the prospects look. (3) Keep your communications clear. (4) Help others to benefit from the multiplier's effects. (5) Let your personal enthusiasm for the job show through. (6) Give your job all you have when the multiplier turns in your favor.

How to Keep in the Mainstream of Progress

Closely related to the benefits from your management personal multipliers is the requirement to keep abreast of developments in your work. In today's lightning-fast, changing world, you can find yourself shunted into the backwater by onrushing events if you fail to gear your managing to this modern stepped-up tempo.

In a large manufacturing plant producing a highly competitive transportation product, Cal Jesup was the manager in charge of pricing and estimating. Cal prided himself on his speed and accuracy in determining costs, calculating emergency safeguards, figuring profits, and coming up with salable price estimates. During a ten-year period of long-run standard products, Cal Jesup built up a strong personal record of being right when he proposed a price.

However, the nature of the product competition changed from two or three large, long-run contracts to several hundred small, short-time-type items. Jesup started coming up with ill-prepared estimates. His price failed to allow enough margin for unexpected contingencies; profits began to suffer.

Orth Fanta, the plant manager, a patient and understanding man, considered the pricing and estimating manager's long record of satisfactory service. He talked with Cal, trying to help, but it only seemed to cause the troubled manager to feel more harassed and greater confusion resulted. Finally, Orth Fanta had to make a change. He removed Jesup and replaced him with a younger manager of much less experience.

This was a real management tragedy, but one which tends to become more and more common as the speed of change, competition, and job complexity increases.

Cal Jesup's management mistakes were: (1) He fell into a rut by failing to recognize the changing requirements of his job. (2) He failed to delegate tasks. He had been successful through his own personal efforts and knowledge. As the job became more demanding, he still tried to handle it in the same old way. (3) Stubbornness robbed him of the help which Orth Fanta tried to give him. (4) He failed to remember that a manager gets his results through others. Remember, you are not hired to do the detail work yourself.

So you should remind yourself that companies. corporations, organizations, and the executives who direct them do not become strong and powerful by simply jealously guarding what they have accumulated, whether it happens to be material goods, personal skills, or a profitable patented process. A most important law for you as you strive to develop your potential as an effective manager is some kind of a constant reminder of your own need for personal growth. You must use your talents, skills, and abilities, or you lose them just as surely as hoarded, inactive money has drastically decreased in value during our time.

Some Benefits When You Read the Signposts Along the Way

Keep on course by knowing how to interpret and apply economic signals to your business.

Ira Stoll was a small precision tool manufacturer. At his plant, The

Precision Die Works, he employed approximately 50 machinists, some of whom were real craftsmen. The proprietor was well-known for quality work, on-schedule delivery, having well-satisfied employees, and also for his astute interpretation of conditions in his industry.

Because of his prominence, a national magazine sent their star business writer, Roger Hamlin, to do a story on The Precision Die Works' success in a highly competitive business. The first thing the writer asked Ira was how he stayed ahead in a field where the competition was so intense that one bad guess could put a small company out of business. Blunt honesty was another of the manufacturer's attributes, and in his reply he agreed that a lot of people yielded to the temptation to make a stab at machine shop work because they thought profits were high and easy to make. However, Ira explained to Roger that these fly-by-nighters failed to realize that to succeed in his business you must know two things: (1) where you are, and (2) where you're going.

Ira went ahead to explain to the writer that he had found that gross national product figures with their components were his best thermometer to the health of the general economy. Mr. Stoll further said that, by tracing these figures back to their source, he had found that they made a pretty good guide as to what was in store for his industry.

Roger Hamlin realized that he was talking with an expert, so he didn't want to interrupt any more than necessary; but he did ask for an example. The manufacturer had one which went like this, "All the spending in the economy can be grouped under one or more of four categories: consumer, capital goods, government, and export. My business is directly affected by the last three, but our best customer is the government defense program. Thus I take a strong interest in the national government's defense budget and keep up with the news which may affect such appropriations. Of secondary importance is capital goods expenditures and exports, since the first is an indicator of general business confidence and the second of foreign sales. They usually represent only 15 to 20 per cent of my total sales."

The magazine writer then asked Mr. Stoll to summarize the guides that he used so effectively. The manufacturer said, "Well, I'd list them this way: (1) an accurate past history of my company, (2) a reliable current measuring stick, (3) the fortitude to use these tools to read my position, good or bad, and (4) the know-how to adjust facts to my current situation." Ira Stoll stated that through using these guides he earned more profit, made calmer decisions, reduced waste, was able to get an early warning of impending trouble, and was braced and ready to meet such difficulties.

As you study Mr. Stoll's guides for managing The Precision Die Works, you should develop some aids which will assist you to stretch your management potential.

How to Get "Go-Confidence"

Company management organization can tend to drift toward centralization of power and authority. Because of this, you should be alert to encourage those reporting to you to apply their own talents freely in accomplishing assigned work. When given just half a chance, in a free choice situation, people will follow "one of the strongest and most creative forces known to man—the attempt by millions of individuals to promote their own interests, to live their lives by their own values." [3]

When you allow the people under your direction to see the personal return to themselves which they can obtain through the application of their own efforts, you are encouraging "go-confidence."

This principle worked out in this fashion for Jon Cray, a third-level manager in the administrative department of a large company. Jon was in his late fifties and carried a lot of responsibility which included employee retirement, insurance, and mechanical communications within the company's facilities. He did an excellent job of managing these important functions with a total of 12 supervisors reporting to him.

Sam George, to whom Jon Cray reported in the organization, realized that Cray's responsibilities could be divided with the mechanical communications being handled by maintenance, insurance by personnel, and retirement by the medical section. Such a rearrangement would not save any money but would contribute to a more orderly assignment of duties. However, Sam George felt that the limited gain from the change could wait until Jon Cray reached retirement age or some unexpected development caused him to terminate his employment.

This delay aroused these difficulties: First, Jon had no future to work for. Even though he was a competent administrator, his experience was totally wrapped up in the sections under his direction. Years of meeting the problems which arose in this assignment enabled him to handle his job almost without effort. This lack of incentive not only curtailed Cray's drive but led to the second problem: It became general knowledge that the department was to be broken up when Jon left, and the subordinate managers were unable to see a future for themselves.

Sam George took the heat out of this twofold dilemma by: (1) *encouraging Jon to contribute some time to community affairs.* The otherwise somewhat bored manager enjoyed the challenge of this kind of service, and it helped to build the stature of the company throughout the local and state areas. (2) *directing Jon Cray to pick out his younger managers with the greatest potential.* These special selectees were given special growth work in their own major areas and were also exposed to the work of other departments.

By thinking, planning, and good management action, Sam George turned a potentially initiative-deadening organizational situation into a growing, go-ahead attention-getter for Jon and a working opportunity for all the managers reporting to him.

You, too, can help give others the go-confidence in any management problem situation if you'll remember that people must have a goal to strive for.

How to Keep Good Employees

As a manager, you can't always pick the way you will travel nor the crisis you'll meet along the way. But try to keep a personal success picture in mind.

You can improve the application of your success-multiplier by studying the experiences of Warren Smaat, a young, first-level manager with seven years of service in a large manufacturing plant. Warren's hard work had attracted favorable attention from his line management right up to the top of his division. In search of a way to develop Warren's potential, the plant top management assigned him to a supervisor's position in an entirely new department. This was a brand-new experimental idea for this large company, and Warren rightly felt highly complimented that he was chosen to inaugurate this practice. However, the road was not to be traveled according to the original plan because a strike developed forcing higher wages in one of the company's other plants, and the shutdown spread to the local operation.

The strike continued on for a long, costly period. When it was finally settled, management at all levels was more concerned with getting production rolling again and trying for a profitable recovery than in the experimental training of an ambitious young manager. The rotation plan which Warren started was abandoned. Thus, what had promised to be an exciting, rewarding growth experience went down the drain. The young supervisor stayed with his job for another full year, during which time he saw no evidence that his superiors were even giving consideration to any ways to help him move up in the organization.

At this time it happened that another large company in a different kind of business sent a recruiter to the university where Warren Smaat was taking night classes on his own initiative for self-improvement. This company's management had a keener appreciation of the value of hiring and developing superior managers. They offered Warren tuition payment for off-regular-hours schooling at a conveniently located university; moving expenses; a rotational and self-development plan, in-plant educational program; and an increase in salary with a review of his progress with his superiors at least annually. This was too good an opportunity to pass up, so the first company lost their valuable investment in an exceptional employee plus the much more profitable services he could have delivered in the years ahead.

Warren Smaat's experience should alert you:

1. Not to neglect your employees with managerial capabilities.
2. To have a visible improvement program.
3. To stimulate all your current managers to encourage self-development by all the employees reporting to them.
4. To put into practice some kind of control system to insure that all managers have their performance reviewed at regular periods.
5. To identify outstanding performers with higher management potential.
6. To find a way to speed the maturing of managers with special abilities.

You will always be confronted with the unexpected in the exciting job of being an out-front manager. This adds a special fascination to your work and tests your mettle. The thing you must do is survive these crises and assist your success-multiplier by reviewing these six fundamentals for practical guidance in choosing the way you should go.

As an ambitious manager, don't overlook the fact that Warren's big opportunity came while he was striving to develop his potential on his own responsibility.

Some Values in Telling Yourself Who's Boss

In endeavoring to multiply your successes and reach your potential, you'll find it helpful to do your job better every day. To achieve this, and stay on the track to a better executive position in business, you must remember that one of the first people you must manage is yourself.

Recently a young executive named Thurman Jance was just beginning to adjust to his demanding, pressure-laden, decision-making position in industry. When he found himself becoming "jumpy," on edge, not sleeping nights, and screaming at the kids at the slightest provocation—being smarter than some colleagues in his profession—he went to see a good doctor. This M.D. gave the manager a thorough examination and told him to stop smoking, reduce his weight by 20 pounds, get regular exercise, and, within a short time, he would find his troubles would disappear.

Thurman Jance listened, but as he went home these thoughts ran through his mind, "I don't like the doctor's advice. Smoking is one of my most pleasant diversions. I'm sure it relieves tensions. Furthermore, I like to eat; and that exercise is for the birds. I wear myself out working in the yard and playing golf over the weekends."

With these rationalizations. Thurman temporarily convinced himself that he could smoke a little less, cut out an extra piece of pie now and then, and do a few push-ups when he had time. But this didn't seem to work because he found his decisions on the job harder to make—his concentration difficult. His relationships with associates and subordinates reached the snapping stage.

In this deteriorating situation, the young executive again showed his intelligence by concluding that it might be a good idea to try the doctor's advice. He broke off smoking, watched his diet, and began regular morning and evening walks. Thurman Jance began to feel better, enjoyed his work more, and found his nerves calming down. He became rather proud of himself because he felt that he was mastering his physical desires. It gave him a new sense of personal power which was reflected in better performance on the job.

The principle which this executive discovered is not applicable to just getting rid of bad habits. It's also useful in building your management skills through controlling your personal emotions, disciplining yourself to meet the difficult problems, and training yourself to make objective judgments which are the basis of better decisions.

So, as a winning success-multiplier, remember to tell yourself who's boss.

SUMMARY

1. Study the total job to be done.

2. Ease troublesome problems by:

    (a)   Knowing where you are going.

    (b)   Benefiting from experience.

    (c)   Maintaining leadership control.

    (d)   Acting on your best judgment.

3.   Test your judgment by:

    (a)   Establishing reliable sources of information.

    (b)   Weighing the opinions of others.

    (c)   Using your full knowledge.

    (d)   Backing your decisions with courage.

4.   Encourage the success-multiplier in your managing.

5.   Keep your managing up to date.

6.   Establish and read the signposts along the way.

7.   Make the best use of available talents.

8.   Recognize good employees.

9.   Be boss of yourself.

NOTES TO CHAPTER 9

[1] Arthur W. Cowles, "Somethin' May Be Gaining on You," *Management News*, Vol. 39, No. 9 (September, 1966), p. 7.

[2] *Wall Street Journal* (Dallas), March 6, 1967. Lee Berton: "Who Needs It?"

[3] Milton Friedman, *Capitalism and Freedom*, Phoenix Books (Chicago: The University of Chicago Press, 1963), p. 200.

10

How to Sharpen Up
Your Know-Ahead
Antenna

Y ou need to anticipate possible problems and take preventive action to avoid errors. You'll not rise very high in your profession unless you have a sense of the future, an ability to prognosticate what will probably happen at some subsequent time as the result of current events and/or actions.

How to Make an Educated Guess about Where You're Going

Norton Wurth, president of Star Fine Mobile Homes, had guided his company to an average annual 12 per cent growth in net profits over the past seven years. The company specialty—luxury-type homes—sold well through the boom period of the Sixties, but Norton detected a definite softening of the market in late 1967. The president reasoned that this condition paralleled the downturn of the leading indicators of general business conditions.

In talking with his sales manager about what should be done, the president received a strong recommendation that the Star line be expanded to include a medium-priced mobile home and camper-type overnight sleepers. However, the manufacturing superintendent objected strongly.

Norton Wurth made this listing:

Pluses:

1. A full product line makes a better impression on the prospective customer.

2. Potential profits would be greater because a variety of choices would offer more flexible competitive price advantages.

3. The camper-type market should benefit from the generally increased leisure time, more vacations, and earlier retirements.

4. Increasing population and a shifting labor force would benefit sales of our medium-priced homes.

Minuses:

1. This change would disrupt a smooth-running production line.

2. The training of new employees, retraining, and shifting of present workmen, represents an uncertain amount of additional cost.

3. New sources of raw material, more floor space and equipment, as well as more employees, would be required.

4. As much as double the current dollar investment is an estimate of the added funds needed.

5. Interest rates are high due to the general economic boom.

Weighted Judgment Considerations:

1. During the general business declines of 1949, 1954, 1958, and 1961, lower-priced homes were in greater demand.

2. The army training base just 25 miles north of Star is to be reactivated before the end of next year.

3. Retained earnings of the company would defray the added costs if my estimate proved reasonably correct.

4. Scheduled cuts in employment by several local industries would provide a choice of workmen to increase our manpower.

On the basis of this analysis Norton Wurth directed the expansion of Star Fine Mobile Homes to include a complete product line as recommended by the sales manager.

In sharpening up your know-ahead antenna to increase your potential as a decision-maker, be sure to detail the pluses and minuses. However, don't stop there; look for the special considerations which cause every important decision you make to be an individual determination.

Failure to take this approach to making management decisions is self-defeating.

Avoid Being Your Own Worst Enemy

Rupert Cornslag inherited a candy manufacturing plant upon the death of his father. He also had some money which he invested in the stock market. He did all right—beginner's luck—which caused him to think he'd really found something, and he made a study of the market. Stock sales' volume on the down- and upside kept him awake nights. Then, as inevitably happens, the market started one of its downward plunges. One of the things Rupert had learned was that common stock prices were a leading indicator of the direction of the general economy; so the candymaker said, "we're in for a depression," and immediately started cutting down on the quality of the ingredients in his candies. He used cheaper grades of sugar and imitation flavorings. He failed to maintain the immaculate shop that had been his earlier trademark and neglected the paint on the building, inside and out. He even became so worried about the coming business decline that he got snippy with his customers, causing them to leave in droves. So things went from bad to worse in the candy shop. Profits vanished, and the proprietor finally had to sell out at less than inventory valuation. Rupert had a depression all right; but at the same time that he was going broke, all the other enterprises in the immediate area were doing well. A clear case in which Rupert had acted as his own worst enemy.

As you project your future in an effort to develop your full potential, remember these guides: (1) Whether you personally feel tip-top or not, and even when your business prospects look dark and uncertain, you should keep in mind that you must intelligently strive to meet and solve your business problems. (2) You should build on your past successes. In Rupert's enterprise, he had the correct formula—good quality, neat and clean shop, and courteous service, as proven by experience—but he took his eyes off his objective, became panicky, and lost his management advantage. (3) You depend upon your customers, so you must treat them with special respect. Whether the person you must please is your boss or individuals outside your organization, you cannot afford to exhibit an unpleasant temper. (4) Your attitude should indicate optimism in the face of all difficulties. Anything less than your best, most confident effort will encourage the same kind of slide backward which Rupert brought upon himself.

Some Values to You in Taking a Closer Look at Business Cycles

In sharpening up your abilities to look ahead, it's important that you know that what we refer to as periods of good business and periods of poor business seem to occur with patterned regularity. These fluctuations of general business, both up and down, are termed business cycles.

In an effort to predict the turning points in business activity, all sorts of statistics, indexes, and even natural phenomena have been studied. Although economists still can't determine with absolute accuracy what changes are in store for business activity before it becomes clearly evident, you can stretch your talents to their higher potentials by making plans based on your judgment of what the future holds for general business activity. Of some help in carrying out this requirement is the information that 26 identified business cycles from 1854 through 1961 have averaged 49 months.[1] On the average, the 26 cycles have lasted 30 months on the upside and 19 months on the downside.

Another fact you should remember is that our present state of knowledge about business cycles indicates that each fluctuation has its own individuality. Since World War II, the recessions have been shorter and milder, lasting only about a year from peak to trough. At times, contractions have been longer than expansions. The first six months have usually been a key. If the drop is rapid, the recession following is severe; likewise, if the initial decline is small, the recession is mild. The rate of rise in the early stages of an expansion has been more rapid after a severe contraction than after a mild one. However, despite a slower rate of expansion, recoveries have generally attained and exceeded previous peak levels much more quickly after mild contractions because the amount of ground to be recovered is smaller than after a severe contraction.[2]

Some ways that knowing more about business cycles can usually help you in effective management are:

1. In getting the most for your money. At the peak of a boom, skilled labor is usually short, prices of materials will be higher, and delivery of machinery will be slower. All of these are important facts for a look-ahead manager to consider in industry or a business of any kind. In the trough of the cycle, the reverse is usually true, where special buying opportunities are often possible.

2. In carrying out your action duties, since decision-making is your stock-in-trade, the better you know general business conditions, the more confidently you can call the shots.

3. To check your progress. If your competitor companies are earning higher profits than your company, you had better look for the source of your problems. The greater the breadth and depth of your knowledge, the more useful it becomes to you since this will assist you to get some special information about regular and prospective suppliers and also your buyers.

How to Appraise Past Business Declines

To get the most benefit from an understanding of business cycles, you must know something about the cause and effects as well as current conditions.

Each cycle has its own special personality. For instance, the 1929-1933 severe decline seems to have been caused by: bank failures, an outflow of gold, the decline of currency in circulation, and a lack of significant action by the Federal Reserve System. Later, in our sharpest economic decline in so short a period of time, during the early months of 1938, the downturn seems to have come about because the banking system's required reserves were raised too rapidly, thus forcing a calling of loans and a reduction of investments, drastically reducing the money supply.

The 1949 recession was heralded as the best advertised in history, but it turned out to be nothing more than an inventory adjustment. As the decline in business started, banking reserve requirements were lowered. Federal Reserve member banks doubled their loans and investments. Short-term loan rates to businesses were reduced. Strength in automobile buying and new housing also helped to offset the adjustment.

The downturn of business in 1954 resulted from a defense spending cutback after the Korean conflict. To spur recovery, reserve requirements were reduced for banks of the Federal Reserve System, discount rates were lowered, and a decrease in the rate of interest on business loans served to encourage an increase in loans and investments. Also, don't overlook the tax cut of 1954. Payments of unemployment insurance and Social Security benefits tended to maintain a stable level of personal income.

In 1958, personal income remained high, but both business and consumers decided to stop their purchases of investment goods at the same time. Inventories were cut, and spending for equipment and new plants was reduced. Ordinary citizens reduced their purchases of autos and durables. The easing of credit, expanded loans and investments, plus the work of the automatic stabilizers, i.e. unemployment payments, Social Security benefits, and reduced tax payments, combined to help lift the economy back on its upward tilt.

Early in 1961, unemployment reached almost 7 per cent of the civilian labor force, and an estimated 20 per cent of the manufacturing capacity was unused. At the end of the year, after an economic turnabout, President Kennedy gave these reasons for the nation's business recovery: (1) the extension of unemployment insurance benefits on a temporary basis; (2) Federal aid made available, through the states, to dependent children of the unemployed; (3) more liberalized Social Security benefits; (4) passage of the home-building Housing Act of 1961; (5) raising of minimum wages and extending it to more workers; (6) through the provisions of Federal aid under the Area Redevelopment Act. The President also credited the Federal Reserve with prompt action to increase the money supply.[3]

How You Can Use the Lessons of the Past in Future Actions

As you use past business cycle history to sharpen up your know-ahead antenna, you must use sound judgment as well as know a lot of facts.

To exploit your full potential as a manager, you must appreciate that ours is a money economy. History repeatedly shows that "as money goes, so goes the state of business." If this commodity becomes tight, interest rates increase, investments and loans are curtailed, spending retreats; then the vitality of trade is retarded just as if a person's individual blood supply should be unexpectedly squeezed down.

So, as a forward-looking manager, one of your first concerns must be to watch the circulating "stuff" we call *money* as you should your own blood pressure.

Here's a manager's learning situation. Hank Stuller was a department manager for The Wireco Company, a relatively small manufacturer of electrical circuits and other components for a large producer of radios and TVs. General business conditions were good:

there was high employment, steadily increasing prices, and full utilization of productive equipment. Hank was enjoying his work. When some of the other managers complained that their budgets were getting a closer scrutiny and that the finance department seemed alarmed about higher interest rates, Hank Stuller passed it off by saying, "That's their job." Stuller told his colleagues that all Wireco expected of him was to get out more and more units per day. To meet his declared goal, Hank daily hired more people, who, because of full employment, required a training period before they could be productive. The department manager contracted for added machinery and equipment to the limit of his authority. These capital goods were not available for immediate delivery because the machine and tool producers were behind with their orders.

With this extended situation in his shop, the department manager was called in for a conference with his superior. The plant manager explained that their bank was insisting upon a substantial loan repayment during the following month and, further, that it was too expensive to secure funds from any other source. So his boss told Hank that he would have to cut back his spending, along with a reduction in all other departments, and that The Wireco Company must conserve every dollar possible. To make sure that his point was understood, the plant manager said, "This means to reduce your payroll to the bare bones at once and cut out all new purchases of tools and equipment. We are also studying our inventory to eliminate as much cost in this area as we can."

With this kind of directive, Hank Stuller knew that he was in trouble. He returned to his office and called in his key subordinates to see just how badly out on the limb he had climbed. The upshot of their review was that 50 people had to be laid off as quickly as policy permitted. In addition, the department manager was forced to pay a contract cancellation fee to his suppliers for equipment on order but on which he could not take delivery.

As a result of these economies, The Wireco Company was able to survive this financial crisis, but there were these aftermaths hanging on for years: (1) Poor labor relations. Skilled people didn't apply for employment. Those who were essential demanded and received a wage in excess of the standard. The local union was progressively harder to deal with because of a strong distrust about how the company might mistreat employees. (2) Suppliers demanded cash or allowed very restrictive short-term credit. (3) Wireco's customers trimmed their order and insisted on prices which permitted only a paper-thin profit.

These are some of the manager's facts of life which you should learn from Wireco's difficulties:

1. Hank Stuller was given more authority than he could properly carry as a limited-ability manager.

2. The plant manager should have done one or more of these things:

   (a) Made a better selection of his subordinate manager.

   (b) Given him better training in the responsibilities of his job.

   (c) Applied some controls earlier to avoid the waste which occurred and the long-range handicaps to The Wireco Company.

3. Some fundamental economics should be a required study for every manager before allowing him to be assigned to a position which by nature requires every possible aid in looking ahead to avoid just such problems as those which plagued Hank Stuller.

There is a proper time and place for everything. At just the right time in the business cycle, Hank Stuller would have been making good decisions and doing the kind of things that managers are paid to decide and to do. For instance, had his actions occurred during a time of underemployment, when there was less than maximum use of machines, tools, and equipment and surplus had pushed prices down, he would deserve a gold star for taking full advantage of the business opportunities available to The Wireco Company.

Benefits in Knowing Where You Are Now

You can help your company grow stronger, increase profits, and improve your own position as a professional manager by: selective hiring of employees, full and efficient use of the most modern tools, and insuring an adequate stock of goods for sale when the market is right.

To meet these requirements, you must know where you are in the business cycle and how your company fits into this general pattern. As you plan for future operations, you must be aware that managers, statisticians, economists, and government officials spend more money, time, and effort in trying to probe the uncertainties of what's ahead of business than any other look-ahead effort.

"I just watch the changes in the price of copper," was the reply of a veteran foundry operator when he was asked how he judged the direction of the general state of business. There are many systems designed to foretell what's ahead for the economy which attest to the importance of this endeavor, such as the National Bureau of Economic Research leading index and their "coincident" and "lagging" indicators. The coincident group moves with the general business cycle, while the lagging index follows the turn in the level of activity. *The National Industrial Conference Board* compiles a principal Diffusion Index and an auxiliary Diffusion Index designed to point out the turning points in business cycles when the aggregate breaks out of a prescribed range.

George Shea, discussing the decline in the price index of raw industrial commodities said, "All 22, according to the Bureau of Labor Statistics of the U. S. Department of Labor, which compiles the index, are 'sensitive basic commodities whose markets are presumed to be among the first to be influenced by actual or anticipated changes in economic conditions.' This sensitivity of the raw industrial index to supply-demand changes gives it some forecasting value. Economists list it among so-called leading indicators, that is, economic statistics whose fluctuations have often in the past preceded changes up or down in the course of general business." [4]

Common stock prices on the New York Stock Exchange are still another measure which many people consider a thermometer of the health of the economy. The sizable group of investors can exercise an influence since they look at these prices and are at the very least psychologically influenced by whether these market prices rise or fall.

What can a manager glean of value from these tools designed to help tell you where you are now? (1) They should convince you of the complexities involved in attempting to predict future business trends. (2) They should acquaint you with some of the available aids which should be helpful in sizing up what is to come. (3) They should encourage you to look for some benchmarks to use in judging the future direction and progress of your own management responsibility.

To develop your potential, you must use every possible avenue to increase your see-ahead ability. You should match principles with your own experiences and follow up on those that prove practical.

How to Apply Look-Ahead Information for Success

If you are successful to a degree in being clairvoyant, this in itself is not enough. You must put to efficient use what you see as future business opportunities. Let's look at the different approach used by two separate company managements as they manufactured a competing product.

The leaders of Company X correctly determined that there was a marked need for an especially designed, lightweight, high-speed train. The company managers properly expected that this revolutionary form of transportation would be an article difficult to manufacture because of the new and special metals, unusual design, and electronic controls. Company X had earned an honored name through many decades of quality service to the mass transportation industry. Against such a background, an inept management under the direction of a president named Willard Scale (who was a third-generation descendant of the company founder) overextended the organization's capabilities. Management greedily attempted to snatch all the orders in a seller's market by guaranteeing delivery of more self-propelled trains than their plants, space, personnel, equipment, and financial resources could support.

When it became clearly evident that more of everything would be required to meet their contract schedule, a wild search was started for subcontract builders. To get takers, Company X made vague promises of future business, gave unsecured financial help, and made loans of their own best managers in order to lure marginal producers into building subassemblies they had originally planned to construct in their own factories. The quality of work from firms who had been badgered into taking Company X's work was substandard right from the start.

In the home plants, there was a shortage of skilled workmen. To meet this need, managers tried to overman the jobs in an effort to get production, but they were frustrated because newly hired people quickly became discouraged by the confusion and quit. Even a 50 per cent overhiring failed to maintain a stable work force.

A surplus of orders and poorly trained workmen snowed the line managers under an avalanche of paper work. The behind-schedule condition grew worse. The limited number of competent managers had to spend so much time in the offices trying to dig out from under the paper that they couldn't take the necessary time to properly direct production. Further, new and only partially trained managers lacked confidence and frankly admitted that they were afraid to act because they might make a mistake.

Some faulty design work began to become apparent, and this cost more money to correct. Naturally, such charges were tacked onto the already skyrocketing expense of production, which caused the financial management of Company X to insist on a 10 per cent raise of the train's price. However, due to all the confusion, nobody was sure that this increase would cover the real total cost of the product. Mr. Scale, in desperation, hired a team of management consultants at a cost of $1,000 per day—an expense which he justified because he said this was the only way they might survive their management mess. This story does not have a happy ending. Efforts to borrow money brought a demand from the banks that top management would have to be changed before they would discuss financial help, and such an adjustment was finally resolved by merging Company X with a stronger company.

Now, let's look at competitor Y. This company started out a little behind X in the production of its train, due to more careful planning. Jeff French, the president and a very astute manager, was never seriously concerned because he knew that he had a balanced management team in depth behind him, all truly modern professionals. The Company Y article was designed to be faster and easier to build. Also, production was carefully compartmentalized for closer control and specialized labor was used to obtain greater benefits. There was no compromise with quality. Mr. French had followed a practice of developing managers for years. Subcontract suppliers knew that they must meet the schedule with a top quality product. Company Y had always been cost conscious and always maintained strong liquid assets. The cost of every component was known down to the last rivet. Naturally, Y was steadily pulling ahead of X in the "best-man" winning style.

What can you learn from this business situation? Try marking some "rights" and "wrongs."

	Right	Wrong
1. Company X should not have ventured into manufacturing this new form of transportation.	___	___
2. Company X acted properly in booking all the orders possible.	___	___
3. Willard Scale should have insisted that deliveries be scheduled in line with Company X capabilities.	___	___
4. The desperation efforts of Company X to enlist the aid of subcontractors was poor management and unethical.	___	___
5. The shortage of manpower and competent management in addition to all Company X's other troubles should have signaled the need to renegotiate price and schedules.	___	___
6. Mr. Scale made a wise move in hiring the management consultant team.	___	___
7. Company Y gained a big business advantage by careful prior planning.	___	___
8. The continuous management development effort paid off for Company Y.	___	___
9. Careful cost and quality control helped Company Y pull out ahead of Company X.	___	___
10. Company Y by using a professional management, balanced approach to its business succeeded where Company X failed.	___	___

These added tips should be helpful: (1) Be sure you can deliver on your commitments. (2) Be fully knowledgeable about your capabilities. (3) Keep your business relationships ethical. (4) Give attention to your administrative duties. (5) Don't try to make competent business managers overnight. (6) Know your costs. (7) Don't get panicky when troubles crowd in on you.

On the ten right-wrong statements, only one through six are wrong; the others are right.

Measures for "How-Am-I-Doing?" Testing

It is valuable to you to be able to check your performance as you sharpen up your look-ahead antenna.

Serge Rollo, a crew supervisor with three years of job experience and a good formal education, had a friend named Ladd Marven, a college graduate with two years on a job which carried parallel authority and responsibility with that of his counterpart in management.

Both managers worked for a high-pressure organization selling life insurance. The duties of each could be defined generally as those intended to generate enthusiasm, give any special assistance to their sales crews, and provide creative ideas to keep the approaches used by their men fresh and productive. It was a situation made to order for a contest between the two groups.

Serge Rollo had an experienced crew and spent most of his time making calls with one after another of his salesmen. It was his practice to listen and, later, when the two were alone, he usually had some suggestions which he made with care to get the right sort of acceptance. By following this formula for an extended period, he was able to: (1) pick out the most effective techniques of each salesman in his crew, (2) help each to improve his style and effectivity, (3) get to know the strengths and weaknesses of every man in his unit, (4) make a much better evaluation of each crew member and thus assure salaries and raises commensurate with the performance of each individual, and (5) use the kind of leadership which produced the best results from each individual.

Ladd Marven also was fortunate enough to have experienced

salesmen. However, his management method was entirely different from that of Serge. Ladd did not have an outgoing personality and had never been particularly successful on the firing line in sales. The boss had picked him as a manager because he had an extremely keen mind and was dedicated to his work, evidenced by his complete lack of hobbies and long hours spent on the job. A cardinal difference between the two was that where Serge Rollo used persuasion to get results, Ladd Marven used a hammer-like approach. For instance: (1) Ladd kept careful records which he reviewed constantly; and, if a man started slipping, that salesman heard about it. (2) When one of his crew did an exceptional job, he was rewarded, usually with an extra-money bonus. (3) Each man was encouraged to go his own way independently, keeping his best techniques to himself. (4) All the members of Ladd's group were given the rough-brush treatment—the attitude being: we want results around here and no fooling around. (5) Ladd never bothered to tell a salesman how he was doing unless it was some bad performance, of course.

Which of the two was the best manager? By the acid test of results, *production* for about a year seesawed back and forth between the two. Then the working atmosphere in the two groups began to take its toll. Turnover in Ladd Marven's crew was quite high and more ulcers were active. Some good producers quit and joined rival companies. In Serge Rollo's group, it was only when a truly outstanding promotion was offered that anyone left voluntarily. As a whole, the people seemed to enjoy their work. Rollo's crew started to consistently turn in better results.

To take advantage of your opportunity to become a better manager, make a note of these points: (1) Over the long pull, in the contest for continuity of higher production, Serge Rollo's method got better results. (2) Ladd Marven's philosophy of management included no allowance for individual differences, while his fellow manager's thinking did recognize this fact. (3) This is not a contrast between so-called *hard* and *soft* supervision. The results obtained prove that Serge used the kind of management best fitted to the individual. When the occasion called for it, he did get tough. (4) Serge's type of management is distinctly more professional and more difficult to master and use than that employed by Ladd. (5) In overall costs, Serge saved his company money. It is expensive to train new employees and doubly so if they join a competitor and use the skills against you that have cost you money to give them. So, to look ahead with clarity, use the type of management which pays off over the long pull.

SUMMARY

1. Develop a sense of the future and keep a clear head on business facts.
2. Don't let false fears limit your vision.
3. Recognize the hazards in business cycle predictions.
4. Learn to appraise past business declines.
5. Apply past lessons to your future actions.
6. Judge and use knowledge of your present position.
7. Strive for balanced management.

NOTES TO CHAPTER 10

[1] *Business Cycle Developments* (September, 1966), p. 65.
[2] Julius Shiskin, "Business Cycle Indicators: The Known and the Unknown," U. S. Department of Commerce (n.d.), p. 9.
[3] *Economic Report of the President* (January, 1962), pp. 5-6.
[4] *Wall Street Journal* (Dallas, Texas), August 8, 1966. George Shea: "The Outlook."

11

How to Be
a Boom Builder

A good manager must be able to size up his situation. To make your contribution to building a boom for your company, to fully utilize effective management techniques, you must retain a reality of viewpoint. You must guard against losing the facility to view your problems from an external perspective.

Avoid Excessive Pressures

Special pressures and stresses are occupational hazards which you must accept as part of your job environment. These tensions are a way of life and good for you if you can handle them. The assignment without stress is one that'll not take you anyplace.

Basic to survival in a challenging management climate is a self-certainty of your own importance. You've got to think well of yourself. Two things will help you get and keep this magic requirement: (1) good decisions, and (2) the ability to draw from a creativity reservoir.

Since most problems you encounter have more than one answer, if pressures make you indecisive, then increased stress will follow. Overwork and fatigue can dull your decision-making powers. In the rough-and-tumble competition in which one manager endeavors to advance his position while another attempts the same thing, egos can be bruised and creativity may be stifled. You must be on guard against these dangers to your career.

Six rules you can follow to help you keep your perspective and avoid the squelch which follows wrong reactions to tensions are:

1. *Put a stress thermometer on yourself* by studying your own reactions leading up to "more than you can take." This is a gauge that only you can handle, and you may have to make a few wrong turns to obtain a foretaste of your approaching "flash point." However, you'll never fulfill your potential for your best future until you are able to read the signs which will help you avoid the squelch.

2. *Give your stretch nerves a rest.* After you have worked out an early warning system for your breakpoint, be sure to dodge stepping over the line by having periodic, daily releases:

    (a) Forget about your work in a stroll around your office, outside your work area.

    (b) Try not to handle regular business at lunchtime.

    (c) Be careful about taking your job home with you.

    Daily breathers can be as important as a two week vacation.

3. *Have a planned program of physical exercise.* This can be very simple, but it must include a regular reaching for your limits even if only briefly. Just as you must stretch for your management potential, the physical reach must be beyond your grasp to tone your "feel-good" needs.

4. *Talk about your problems.* This is not with the thought of getting back answers but rather to clarify your own thinking. You'll be

surprised at how frequently this can uncover a solution and whisk away the stress. You'll do better to choose a confidante who doesn't feel compelled to attempt to give you a solution. A listener is what you need.

5. *Put each step in its proper slot.* It relieves the pressure to know that you are following a well-defined plan to meet your problem:

    (a)   Identify the parts.

    (b)   Consider alternatives.

    (c)   Define an action.

    (d)   Do something about the difficulty.

    (e)   Check back for final results.

6. *Lean on a physician in whom you have confidence.* Select a good doctor and follow his advice. Follow a realistic diet with regular eating habits. See that you get enough thorough checkups to catch any physical malfunctions and to insure that you can enjoy the peace of mind which comes with confident good health.

By following this six-step pattern, you'll make your decisions without the stress handicap penalty. From this vantage point, you can concentrate your full attention upon the problem to be solved. This releases a greater creativity which can be easily blunted by not preparing to meet the normal tension which every manager must face.

As you pursue the objective of helping to guide your company to more, better, on-schedule production at lower and lower costs, after setting up a bulwark against having your freedom to operate squelched, you must give attention to some further dangers.

Side-Step the Manager's Triple-Threat Handicap

These threatening barriers are really temptations which can cause you to take the wrong course. The first of these dead-end streets that you must dodge is a *suspected advantage which invites you to be unethical.* Your natural drive to win a more profitable advantage for your company can make it very desirable to manipulate the shifty trio: demand, supply, and price. It is important to control this competitive urge.

When the desire and opportunity to be unethical becomes evident, remind yourself of this fact: When a manager works as hard to succeed legitimately on his job as he must to try to gain an unfair advantage, he'll come out better the honest way every time.

When you develop your talents and strive to build a boom for your company, you'll avoid any suspicion of unethical practice. These offshade actions do not have to be a big thing like illegal price fixing, limiting production, or dividing territory. You weaken your leadership any time you lessen the confidence of employees under your direction. Even a seemingly small thing like using a subordinate's idea without giving him credit can cut the effectiveness of your management control.

You'll do better for yourself and the company to follow a code of honesty, right practices, and on-the-job ethics.

A second, frequently experienced handicap is the *temptation to take the easy way*. You can't encourage a boom for your company by taking the easy course. Among the contributions you must make to do your part to assure an upward tilt of the progress curve are to: (1) Provide as many jobs as efficient at productive work. (2) Make wise investments in capital goods. (3) Develop new and better ways to increase quality production. (4) Encourage and meet effective demand. (5) Do everything you can to maintain stable prices.

You can get some tips from the experiences of Ralph Crano, a first-level manager on the heat-treat operation of The Mechano Company, a manufacturer of auto bus bodies. Crano, a veteran manager, was able to make one of his operating principles stick: this was that every new man hired to work in his section must have training in attaching the honeycomb support material to the body sheet steel before the unit was trucked into the furnace. In the face of strong union pressure to have this training done on the job, Ralph held firm and thus gained the advantage of being able to devote all his attention to productive work.

When the manufacturing research department of The Mechano Company proposed a plan for purchasing a line of three sequenced heaters for his section, Ralph countered with a suggestion for an entirely new kind of furnace which allowed the curing process to be done at three levels. Some of the advantages of the manager's suggested equipment were that it was much less expensive to purchase and install, it did not require any additional floor space, it could be operated with the same number of men, and it gave a directly constant and more easily controlled heat with a greatly reduced possibility of varied quality. By stressing these advantages, Ralph Crano was able to sell his idea.

Not only was Crano on the job with good ideas for new equipment, but also he had another commendable practice which was to take time to carefully read and study all the distributors' and sales' reports, giving special attention to comments of customers. When he read something which was not clear to him, he wrote those involved for further information. Over the years, Ralph had built up a free and easy kind of back and forth communication so that salesmen and dealers frequently stopped in the factory to discuss ideas and suggestions they had picked up for possible improvements.

As a real boomer for his company, when wage-bargaining time came around Ralph was always a member of the management negotiating committee. He had so many facts and figures on every phase of his operation, that the final agreement between union representatives and management was reached in an amicable fashion with fairness so that few prices had to be increased.

You can help keep your business boom alive if you remind yourself that Ralph Crano did not build his successful position in management by taking the easy course. He worked at his job, demonstrated patience, used intelligence and judgment, and took some chances to win a solid position as a leader.

A third temptation of which you must beware is that of *treating employees with less than the dignity to which they are entitled.*

Cary Elfin was the manager of the lens-grinding operation of the Standard Vision Company, a good-sized optical equipment producer. One of the skilled technicians reporting to the manager was a talented young fellow named Brit Long. A significant series of incidents started when Brit discovered a simple attachment for his machine which would give a smoother finish to the lenses and triple the output from each machine. The skilled workman demonstrated his improved process to his superior; and he, in turn, passed it on up the line. Brit received a substantial money award for his alertness and was recognized as Process-Improvement Man of the Year. The quality-finishing, cost-saving device was installed on all the grinders, permitting a worthwhile lowering of production costs.

Cary Elfin was the kind of manager who would go to almost any ends to get favorable recognition from his superiors. Brit's award and publicity properly reflected credit upon Cary, and thus the manager started putting pressure on the other workmen to come up with usable ideas for improvement.

By constantly harping upon the need for production improvements, Cary upset his crew, reduced production, and failed to learn of any new processing methods. Worse than this, the boss' arm-twisting and harassment aroused so much resentment that a majority of the employees joined a union which had tried unsuccessfully for years to obtain bargaining rights for Standard Vision Company employees.

This resulted in higher wage costs, made the company less competitive, and made Cary Elfin's job more difficult: all because he failed to treat the people reporting to him with the dignity to which they were entitled.

To make your contribution to the boom for your company, you should be watchful of the old wives' tales, such as, "A manager has the duty, obligation, and right to involve himself in a subordinate's personal affairs." Even a partial acceptance of this fallacy causes more lost time through idle chitchat and prattling than any other energy-waster. Remember this: You may carefully, *with judgment*, endeavor to help an employee if drinking, debts, women, or whatever the weakness may be is clearly interfering with his job performance.

A second maxim which can be harmful is: "Praise to the limit." With respect to this operating adage, it is O.K. if you are careful to place honesty as a first essential. You have no right to waste this superior motivator by overuse when commendation is not deserved. Use brief compliments specifically to the point. Spontaneity is most effective as a measure of when to act. Remember this: Don't exaggerate; be specific; give with enthusiasm; and don't attempt to keep your praise a secret.

A third management tradition widely believed is: To rise through the organization, all an ambitious employee needs is hard work, an understanding of his environment, to be aggressive, demonstrate honesty, and the ability to keep his head under pressure.

Remember this: The key to success for you is how others react to your leadership. The kind of a job that subordinates do will make or break your future progress in your profession.

To build a more successful management career for yourself, you need to know and practice the principles of good personal relationships. This means that you must: (1) Treat all employees with respect. (2) Avoid any tinge of favoritism. (3) Get an awareness among the people reporting to you that real wage increases are only possible in proportion to the rise in productivity. Remember, you will be promoting a boom for your company if you are able to use your management strengths to accomplish these ends and avoid the previously mentioned destructive handicaps.

How to Get on the Right Side of Your Problems

Another of your important areas of responsibility is problem solving; and, if you get started correctly, you'll get better results. In solving management problems, most often getting started right means that you look for the key people in your difficulty.

Management as a profession has come a long way from almost 100 years ago when imaginative promoters thought only of immediate profits. They generally saw no reason to know or care what employees thought, and lived every day as if it would be the last opportunity to swindle another through dishonest or at least morally questionable tactics.

That you can still operate in an environment that allows a can-do system's principles to survive and flourish in spite of such abuses is a tribute to the fundamental soundness of our economic way of life.

You can cultivate the boom and extend your potential if you are willing to bring yourself up to date.

The Mayfair Company manufactured go-cart racers. In preparation for the annual international meet held at Sutherland's Drag Strip, a popular race course about 100 miles from the plant near the center of the state, Lon Booth, Mayfair's general manager, called in A, B, and C, the managers of the plant's three main divisions.

This was a typical assembly line operation. A directed the building of the frames, B installed the motors, and C painted and finished the cars.

Lon Booth told his key managers, "During the international meet, our salesmen have orders to sell hard every day. I want to get as many of our carts on the track as possible, so I'll see that the best producing department gets a bonus."

On returning to their respective departments, A told his crew, "In the upcoming races we have an opportunity to get the company some good advertising, so I want you to make sure we don't put out any faulty cars. An accident could cause trouble, and so you must make quality a first consideration."

B told his crew, "I've just talked with the big boss and he wants production. And we're going to give it to him. Anyone caught loafing gets laid off. There'll be no visiting around. If you run out of work see me. When I have some more instructions, I'll give them to you."

C appealed to his crew for their ideas to get greater efficiency. As a result, sandblasting, chromating, and painting were rearranged. An extra sander was installed to permit two lines of cars to be finished at the same time.

Now several significant things happened: (1) A's crew became so quality-minded that output was drastically reduced. (2) B had his crew so badly shaken up and scared that they worked as if they had all thumbs, made foolish mistakes, experienced high absenteeism, and generally bottlenecked the few production parts that A's outfit gave them. (3) C was all geared up to put out go-carts in record numbers, but he couldn't get enough racers to keep his crews working efficiently.

Check the ideas on this list which you think will help Lon Booth get on the right side of this problem:

1. Manager A should have relaxed the quality standards.   ____

2. Manager B should have been given some lessons on how to get along with people.   ____

3. Manager C should have been stopped from making the changes until they were needed for increased production.   ____

4. Lon Booth should have more clearly spelled out what he wanted A, B, and C to do.   ____

5. Lon Booth should have followed up after his meeting to check the results of his meeting with A, B, and C.   ____

6. The best producing department should not have been promised a bonus.   ____

The key to getting on the right side of this problem is number five. Each of the other suggestions can be discussed with some values pointed out, but as an effective manager remember your success in building a boom depends upon the responses you get from the people reporting to you.

In striving to stretch your potential, you'll make the greatest gains as you improve your ability to encourage and influence others.

How to Give Good Directions

Most of the time you pay your way by the quality of your leadership rather than the quantity. To get the full benefit of effective management techniques, you need to set some performance standards for yourself.

Keep the mark of your own personality in your managing, but these general guidelines will prove helpful: (1) Decisions concerning your job should never be casually made. (2) Consider the reactions of those reporting to you before you act. (3) Subordinates respond favorably to your interest in what they are doing. (4) Risk overinforming people rather than keeping them in the dark. (5) Be generous when your help is needed.

You can get your organization into big trouble quickly if you disregard these five watch-fors.

The Beach Clam Company, a New England concern, canned a

new health food. This was a blended natural clam meat with added vitamins. The management organization was limited to a president who handled sales, a factory manager who also bought materials, and a director of the work force. The small operation moved along smoothly until the product started catching on and requests came in for fruit-flavored clam meat.

This posed these problems: whether to prepare the fruit juices in-plant or outside, how the flavor should be added, the capital equipment necessary to meet this demand, and how much to raise prices.

The president and his two subordinates decided to buy the fruit and process the juice internally. Money was borrowed for a new conveyor and an attachment which added the juice to the cans just before they were sealed. Figuring the additional costs, they decided that about 5 cents more per can ought to bring them out about right on the new clam meat products.

The factory manager helped with the installation of the new equipment, and then left the director of the workmen to train the newly hired people while he took a trip out of town to see about another source of supply for clam meats and fruits.

On the day that the president had scheduled a visit of key distributors to see the new equipment in operation, the green employees hit the wrong button and threw the conveyors, cans, juices, and meats in all directions. Shortly after this incident, housewives began to complain about mislabeled cans, and sales began to slip. This caused each of the three managers to ask himself where he could have done a better job.

The president should have: (1) checked the problems of adding fruit juices to their product, (2) explored the sales values of this change more fully, (3) been more concerned about the price of the changed product, and (4) kept his subordinates better informed.

The factory manager should have: (1) taken more seriously his material buying responsibilities, (2) helped to get the new equipment operating successfully, (3) offered more advice on the prices to be charged for the new product, and (4) more closely coordinated what he was doing with the other two key managers.

The director of the work force should have: (1) asked for the advice and management counsel he needed, (2) insisted upon having a say-so in the price increase, (3) worked at the job of getting better communication with his fellow managers, and (4) learned more about what the president and factory manager were doing.

You might think of some more *should-have-dones* for these managers. However, the president knew enough about the "watch-fors" that he called a halt to all production while the three managers got their heads together. As a result, a thorough market research study was made, and the equipment manufacturer's mechanics spent sufficient time in the factory to insure that the conveyors and machines were operating properly. The Beach Clam Company machinists were trained to maintain the equipment. After careful analysis, it was determined that the company's interest could best be served by holding to the original price per can. Then the company started back into business and is now progressing satisfactorily.

You can benefit by recognizing that the greatest long-range benefit to come from this serious business problem was a better understanding by each of the three key managers of the five "watch-fors" which would keep them from using sloppy directional practices in the future.

Help Good Employees Retain a Forward Look

You are and should be most interested in your best performing employees. These are the people who see something in their jobs which they value. Many times, it's a brighter future. As a successful manager, you must encourage this enthusiasm.

If you've let your dreams slip away, if hope is gone, if you no longer look ahead, if the fires of your ambition have gone out— then, brother, you are through.

Select the following statements in one, two, three order which you think will best help management-type people develop themselves.

1. Set an example by emphasizing the professional nature of your job.
2. Let him know, in the right way, how he is handling the assignment.
3. Assist him with counsel when the going gets rough.

4. Let him feel the excitement of success and the disappointment of failure.

5. Take the initiative in securing proper wage payments.

6. Don't let outstanding work go unnoticed.

7. Let him in on the know.

8. To the degree that it is practical, practice general supervision rather than the close detailed type.

9. Search for and use the things which are important to your outstanding comers.

10. Be sure that he knows why good work discipline is important.

11. Urge him to set some goals for himself.

12. Be a buffer from harmful opposition, internal or external, when good judgment dictates such protection.

This list can best be applied to a specific individual's needs—just another reason why it's important to know your key subordinates as well as possible. However, as a general application, this will usually turn out to be the most applicable priority order: 1, 4, 11, 9, 2, 6, 8, 3, 7, 10, 12, 5.

All 12 of these actions are valuable motivators, so don't be misled into believing that those lower on the list are not important.

SUMMARY

1. Get an objective feel for your total situation.

2. Avoid excessive pressures.

3. Dodge the triple-threat handicap:

   (a) Beware of the temptation to be unethical

   (b) Don't look for the easy way

   (c) Recognize the dignity of employees.

4. Get on the right side of your problems.

5. Give good directions.

6. Help good employees retain a forward look.

12

How to Use Incentives
for a Payoff

How you handle incentives is important in determining your win or lose results as you strive to get that better job. In helping others, don't get carried away. Remember that our productive economic system is made possible because large numbers of individuals find the incentive to work hard in their own interests, and each has been rewarded on the basis of his useful production as determined by an impartial, unfeeling, and disciplined market.

Some Lessons to Be Learned in Helping Others

You must remember that: (1) Some people, by reason of age, health, and intelligence, cannot fully compete in today's fast-moving productive society. (2) Some people have sufficient capacity that, with proper education and/or training, they can establish a place for themselves and make their full contribution to the progress of your company and to the total economy.

Realism at all times is the keystone in the use of effective management techniques. At no other place is this more essential than when you are attempting to help others.

Frank Charleson was a first-level manager for The Flosoft Company, a rubber-based plastic processing plant of a large rubber goods manufacturer in Ohio. Among other duties, Frank supervised the work of two employees whose assignments included gathering and disposing of the residue scraps from a line of refining machines. In addition, these two workmen trucked finished production to the scales for Frank to weigh before it was stored for shipment. One of these workmen, Bill Newland, was alert, intelligent, and physically strong. The other, Larry Conklin, was dull, unintelligent, and physically below par.

By good management ingenuity, a system of conveyors was developed which disposed of the refiner's scrap and transported, weighed, and delivered the finished production to railroad cars for shipment.

Frank Charleson gave Larry Conklin the relatively simple job of stacking the finished slabs of plastic in railroad freight cars. However, it quickly became apparent that the irregular flow of production caused Larry to become confused, and his performance became erratic. The stock piled up, the ricks in the car fell over, and the former trucker threw up his hands in complete frustration. The next job Conklin tried was sorting scrap, but he was unable to judge which material could be reprocessed. Also, the outside work had an adverse effect on Larry's health.

In an effort to find something the displaced employee could do, the janitorial section gave him a minimum number of rest rooms to service and keep clean. Here, too, more judgment was required than Larry could generate. In addition, he resented the slightest criticism; if a shortage of supplies was called to his attention or a comment was made about the cleanliness of the room, he used this as a reason to take three or four days off. When this absentee record became imposing, Larry Conklin was removed from the payroll.

Bill Newland, the other displaced employee, was given a practice trial on the refining machines where he showed such promise that Frank Charleson placed him in the training activities he used for new operators.

After two weeks' instruction and practice, Bill Newland stepped up to the job of refiner operator with confidence and pride in his ability; and by the end of six months, he was one of the best refining craftsmen in The Flosoft Company.

As you stretch yourself for that higher management job, you'll find that you face many such difficult judgment decisions which vitally concern the people reporting to you. In operating with realism and as a true professional, you must observe these guidelines:

1. What is the best interest of your company?
2. How many people will your decision affect?
3. Are you being entirely fair with the employees directly concerned?
4. Is there an alternative which needs further thought?

When you tailor your actions to these general principles, they will help you meet one of today's growing major management challenges. You must continually remind yourself that, more than any other one thing, your success as a manager hinges upon how well and efficiently you use the people under your direction.

Your best approach is to lay everything out on top of the table in dealing with others. Even if you have a tough personnel problem, face it—that's your job. You'll: (1) gain the respect of those people reporting to you as well as your associates, (2) be protecting your own position and adding security to the jobs of your entire crew, (3) encourage an honest, understandable, and productive working atmosphere, (4) be doing your part to keep the total United States economy as a world business leader.

How to Counter the 25 Per Cent
Wrecker Threat

Just as you need to learn as much as you can about motivating others as you strive to reach your potential, you also need to avoid some of the dangers which are sometimes hidden. You can find yourself at a disadvantage in your managing if you fail to clearly identify what is or can interfere with your professional efficiency.

One of these threats is hidden payroll costs. "Fringe benefits, once merely the icing on the cake, now cost the American businessman a staggering $75 billion plus each year—nearly four times as much as the dividends paid stockholders. What's more, fringe benefit costs are shooting up almost twice as fast as wage rates, according to a comprehensive (1965) industry survey...." [1]

In addition to the danger that you may add an unknown burden to your own employee costs, there is the possibility that a competitor may gain a special advantage because many of his charges in this area are hidden and impossible for you to obtain.

To arm yourself to meet the fringe benefit threat, *first*, recognize that this cost on the average now represents 25 per cent of the all-industries employees' per week earnings. *Second*, fringes in order of costs per employee per week on the average are:

a. paid vacations
b. nongovernment pensions
c. insurance (all types)
d. OASDI
e. paid holidays
f. paid time not worked
g. unemployment
    compensation taxes
h. profit-sharing payments
i. workmen's compensation
    payments
j. paid sick leave
k. employee meals furnished free
l. employee discounts on goods
    and services
m. other fringes

Third, in planning for additions to your payrolls and for overtime work, in considering the utilization of new machinery and equipment, and in trying to anticipate what a competitor may do, be sure that you do not overlook the fringe benefit costs as a factor for careful consideration.

How You Can Slow Down Some Hidden Costs

In Mark Twain's *Adventures of Tom Sawyer*, Aunt Polly effectively used a silken thread and a chunk of burning firewood to remove Tom Sawyer's loose tooth when he attempted to use this molar's alleged ache as an excuse to stay out of school. You may have frequently thought that the threat of some direct, strong, and drastic action such as that taken by Aunt Polly would be good for a malingering employee who has upset your plans by not showing up for work. But, naturally, this is a course of action not open to you.

Managers often become a little bit disgusted to see the unemployment statistics hiked because some prima donna workman will not take what he considers a menial, want-ad type job—even temporarily.

Remember, however, that emotional control is one of the marks of a successful manager. So stretch your potential and score points for yourself by know-how control in three significant areas:

1. *Paid Sick Leave*

   Sick leave becomes a cost and production burden when employees begin to feel that they should use it just because it's there. You are handicapped in controlling this fringe benefit because it is difficult to determine whether an employee is faking or not. So, to discourage the chiseler and to reward the conscientious employee, it is well to study a plan for payment of unused sick leave. This might take the form of an addition to retirement income or a Christmas bonus. Whatever method you decide to use should be carefully checked for a comparison of costs and expected returns. When you work out a plan along this line, suitable to your needs, you'll find the abuses disappear.

2. *Compensation Cases*

   Good managers do not try to duck the cost of injury to an employee for whom the company has a responsibility. However, some people try to get something for nothing and make it difficult for both honest employers and employees. So, when an accident occurs, you should:

(a) See that the injured employee is taken care of.

(b) Make a thorough written report of all the details.

(c) Look into the job history of the individual and the machine and/or job assignment.

(d) If your management position warrants it, work with your compensation commission.

(e) Strive to build a relationship with employees which will enable both the company and workmen to confidently receive what each is entitled to get.

3. *Unemployment Payments*

Under the States' unemployment merit rating plan, you can help to cut your company's costs by:

(a) More careful planning for hiring needs.

(b) More effective use and training of your current employees.

(c) Studying new and better methods of operation.

(d) Keeping up to date on the latest machines and thinking about how they might be used to further production.

(e) Keeping yourself informed about how much your company is paying for this fringe benefit.

You should be aware that many of the fringe costs have had their inception because of careless management by someone. Excessive travel time, long breaks for coffee and smokes, encouraged visiting, unnecessary payment for breakfast and lunches, and limiting of the scope of a job assignment are examples of bad work habits which, when allowed to continue, become accepted as standards for job practices.

Weak supervision is one of the first things that chiselers look for. Thinking back on your own experiences, no doubt you'll remember that on a new assignment one of the first things those reporting to you tried was to search for your soft spot as a manager. So you should always remember to recognize the chiselers; be sure you give and get a fair day's work. This will enable your company to provide the incentive of a fair day's wages—one of the best motivators. A guaranteed wage without personal effort provides little encouragement to an individual to develop his potential.

How You Can Put a Production Base Under Wages

The substantially higher real wage level of the American workman is only possible because these individuals have been able and willing to produce more goods per hour worked.

Your opportunities to supply the urge to produce in those employees reporting to you is handicapped by inflation, by artificial restrictions which prevent your using the incentives you have found to be effective. For instance, government-imposed minimum wage exerts inflationary pressures and makes proper incentives more difficult to use.

The only way that you can safely put a floor under wages and avoid destroying the payoff incentive is if: (1) you can produce sufficient wanted goods and/or services to support arbitrary wage levels, (2) you can achieve enough economies to enable you to continue a profitable business, (3) you are willing to apply the additional and essential know-how to meet these wage levels, and (4) the owners of your enterprise are willing to continue an investment which may yield less than they have been receiving or than they may safely obtain elsewhere. Thus, it is obvious that a compulsory minimum wage places heavier demands upon your time and talents.

How to Answer Some General Alarm Bells

In applying effective management techniques, part of your effort in earning a promotion must be directed toward avoiding some common pitfalls into which a manager can easily slip.

You, like most other good managers, have an urge to do the things which cause others to think well of you. It's a nice warm feeling to get repeated assurances from those reporting to you that they like you. However, in this area you must be careful because you are treading on dangerous ground.

In a large manufacturing plant, Chet Billings was a department head with three subordinate managers, each of equal rank, reporting to him. One of them was a soft-soaper; everything the boss did was just great. Chet had more than his share of egotism, so the subordinate poured it on and the superior repeatedly picked the better assignments for his pet. With the subordinate telling Chet that he was always right in his judgment choices and that his decisions showed a grasp of understanding far beyond his current level of responsibility, the boss raised his outwardly adoring subordinate's pay, added a glowing write-up to his personnel record, and talked about the subordinate's excellent performance to not only his associates but to his superiors as well.

The department head went so far overboard that he promised his fair-haired boy that the very next promotion would be given to him. As invariably happens, the subordinate began to, lightly at first and then more directly, put the squeeze on his indulgent boss. The subordinate started setting his own working hours and missed some important meetings because, as he said, "Something more pressing came up." The favored supervisor assumed authority outside the scope of his job. He even started telling his equals how to handle their assignments. Too late, after he had created a Frankenstein, Chet, the would-be "good-Joe" manager, realized that he had more than he could carry. He didn't hear the alarm bell.

These are the things which Chet Billings did wrong: (1) He was too much concerned with gaining the approval of those reporting to him. (2) He lacked the leadership discernment to recognize that the subordinate was deliberately blinding him with gross flattery. (3) He failed to study his subordinates and evaluate their capabilities. (4) He did not take action to restore discipline and proper management relationships when it became obvious that serious trouble was brewing.

Be on the alert to avoid making similar management errors.

Here's an alarm bell of a different kind: Sales manager Marty Hayes of the Sparks Equipment Company was a good friend of the president of the Uslow Manufacturing Company. The Sparks Equipment Company was a distributor of automatic floor sweepers, generators, electric and gasoline powered scooters. While this was quality machinery, Larson Kune, the Uslow Company president, did see that Marty supplied all their needs for these items, thus making this account by far the most lucrative of any held at the Sparks Equipment Company.

Marty Hayes personally handled the Uslow Company business. His salesmen—A, B, and C—were left on their own to try to cultivate some added business markets. A had wonderful potential; but when nobody paid much attention to him, he became discouraged and joined another firm. The sales manager didn't hurry to replace him. When his superior asked what he was doing about someone to fill A's spot, he told his boss that he was looking around.

B, also, was a good salesman and he, too, started putting out some feelers to see if he couldn't find a more challenging job. C, a different type of employee, wasn't ambitious and was content to collect his monthly fixed wage. He did just enough work to assure this payment but didn't strive for any bonus.

At about this time, Larson Kune saw what he considered an opportunity in real estate; so he resigned from the Uslow Company. The new president had met Marty Hayes but was the kind of an executive who required a salesman to convince him of the value of his product. The long period of easy business living had softened Marty; so the Sparks Equipment Company's share of the Uslow Manufacturing Company's requirements dwindled rapidly and, within six months, disappeared entirely. Thus Marty Hayes, as well as B, was soon looking for another job. C is still hanging on but undoubtedly will be found out later.

The detrimental effect of having only a single buyer is comparable to a manufacturer relying upon a single source for vitally needed material or components. Both are alarm bells.

In using effective management techniques, don't: (1) spend all your time developing a relationship with the president of one company; (2) fail to remember that business friendships should be encouraged, but the product or service you sell must always be able to stand on its own feet when compared with what a competitor has to offer; (3) neglect to help your subordinates grow in their profession; (4) depend too much on your own personal efforts for acceptable sales productivity; (5) blindly drift along with only one purchaser who holds the power to make or break your company; (6) fail to appreciate the danger of a single purchaser and the essentially tenuous hold this gives you. You can wreck your organization and lose your potential for a comeback.

In a third-alarm-bell situation, the employees' union demanded that the Trimline Mower Company provide retirement at 60 with a minimum monthly pension of $150 for all employees with ten years' service. This largesse was to be graduated upward, based upon individual earnings and seniority. The Trimline Company president, a man named Sherman Farmer, was sympathetic because he had come up through the ranks and was a former union steward.

In spite of the advice of his other officers against agreeing to this costly claim, Sherman insisted upon granting the union's demands. The president justified his action on the strength of Bruce Chinnley's (the union business agent) assurance that the men had promised to increase output enough to offset the added cost.

However, instead of increasing production, the workmen actually put forth less effort because they all began to plan what they would do when each reached retirement age and started living on the nice, big, fat pension which had been squeezed out of their employer.

To improve your performance by the use of incentives for a payoff, it is of value to ask yourself: How does a manager get himself into such untenable situations?

Sherman Farmer: (1) allowed misplaced loyalty to an ideal to exercise too strong an effect upon his management decisions; (2) took the counsel of Bruce Chinnley, an outsider with an axe to grind, over the advice of his own team of managers; (3) failed to carefully assess whether the Trimline Mower Company could afford the demanded "giveaway" and what it might expect in return.

After studying these problem situations, you should be increasingly alert to the dangers presented to your management position if you permit your desires for overfriendly relationships to:

1. Create personal debts which can wreck your future professional standing.

2. Box you in with a single market outlet or a single supply source.

3. Overstimulate your charitable impulses without an equitable return for the value of the assets to be given away.

4. Overlook that your subordinates are not growing in their jobs.

How to Use Security for the Best Results

In using incentives for a payoff, don't forget people's universal desire to have some safeguard against future economic wants. Most people work as employees and in varying degrees are concerned about what would happen to them and their dependents if their jobs should be lost.

Historically, 4 per cent unemployment in the United States is not unhealthy. This is based upon the recognized need for mobility in our working force. To meet the requirements growing out of a business system in which workmen must be able and willing to move from a place of low employment to another where jobs are available, a willingness to change the kind of work and upgrade working skills is also an essential.

An increasing burden on taxpayers is that of providing support for people who don't work. If welfare payments or other nonwork benefits hinder this flow of employees into and out of jobs as the real needs require, then: (1) Personal initiative is stifled. (2) People tend to lose their individuality. (3) Waste and indolence is encouraged. (4) These giveaway programs become more and more popular, spread out, and expand. In some communities, three generations are living on relief. It can become a way of life.

To manage better and offset the growth of unearned welfare payments, you must: (1) Convince yourself that the urge for security is a normal human desire. (2) Understand that you and everyone else in the nation can have more only if more can be produced with greater efficiency. (3) Make better use of the people, materials, tools, machines, and money at your disposal.

Some Tips on How to Build a More Secure Future

If you ask a representative group of employees what they want from their job, you'll probably get as many different answers as there are people responding.

However, after careful analysis, these replies divide themselves into two broad categories: *first,* concrete or material returns; and, *second,* satisfaction of intangible hopes or desires.

In fulfilling the requirement in the number one grouping, you need to give attention to:

1. Making your own and your subordinate's job exciting.

2. Assuring that the evident importance of the work sticks out sharply and clearly.

3. Letting the wage and salary payments reflect the value of the contribution of the work.

4. Facing up to an employee's right to know how he is doing on the job.

5. Encouraging a subordinate's peace of mind by stimulating his participation in planned savings, his own pension plan, sufficient insurance, and hospitalization.

To meet the less concrete, but equally important, needs of a self-respecting employee, you must:

1. Encourage and provide on-the-job opportunities for personal growth.

2. Help him contribute to community improvement.

3. And, closely related to number two, assist your subordinates to enjoy a healthy social relationship with others.

4. Promote a sense of freedom by providing your subordinate with decision-making situations, a chance to develop his desire for self-responsibility, and opportunities to exercise personal discipline and thus secure the rewards of success.

SUMMARY

1. Emphasize self-help in assisting others.

2. Use knowledgeable support to stimulate others.

3. Offset the costs of fringe benefits.

4. Strengthen your management and watch hidden costs.

5. Promote production to offset wage costs.

6. Look out for complacency.

7. Use better productivity as the key to greater security for all.

To Step Through the Success Door
by Using Effective Management Techniques

DO THIS: Study your profession for get-results powers.

DO THIS: Learn how money; jobs; supply, demand, and price; and aggressiveness can help you display your qualifications as a manager.

DO THIS: Practice look-ahead skills as you sharpen your know-how to fit that bigger job in management.

NOTES TO CHAPTER 12

[1] Jack Wooldridge, ed., "Fringe Benefits—Now Rising Twice as Fast as Wages," *Nation's Business*, Vol. 54, No. 8 (© August, 1966), pp. 50-52.

BIBLIOGRAPHY

Burck, Gilbert, "The Auspicious Rise of the Soviet Consumer,"
pp. 132-133. *Fortune*, August, 1966. Chicago: Time Inc.

——, "The Toughest Management Job in the World," pp. 74-77.
Fortune, Vol. LXXIV, No. 1, July 1, 1966. Chicago: Time Inc.

Business Cycle Developments (September, 1966), p. 65. Washington, D. C.: U. S. Department of Commerce, Bureau of the
Census.

Cowles, Arthur W., "Somethin' May Be Gaining on You," p. 7.
Management News, Vol. 39, No. 9, September, 1966. New
York: American Management Association, Inc.

Dommermuth, William P., "On the Odds of Becoming Company
President," p. 72. *Harvard Business Review*, May-June, 1966.
Boston: Harvard Business Review.

Drucker, Peter F., *Managing for Results*, pp. 60-61, 226-227. New
York: Harper & Row, 1964.

Dubin, Robert, *Human Relations in Administration*, 2nd ed., p. 51.
Englewood Cliffs, N. J.: Prentice-Hall, Inc., © 1961.

Economic Report of the President (January, 1962), pp. 5-6. Washington, D. C.: United States Government Printing Office.

"Europe Takes a Tip—from U. S. Businessmen," p. 72. From a copyrighted article in *U. S. News & World Report*, January 16, 1967.
Washington, D. C.: U. S. News & World Report, Inc.

Evans, Marshall K., "A Corner on the Creativity Market," pp. 36-37.
Advanced Management Journal, Vol. 32, No. 1, January, 1967.
New York: Society for Advancement of Management.

First National City Bank, *Monthly Economic Letter*, pp. 92-95.
August, 1965. New York: First National City Bank.

Friedman, Milton, *Capitalism and Freedom,* Phoenix Books, p. 200. Chicago: The University of Chicago Press, 1963.

Fusfeld, Daniel R., "The Manpower Revolution," pp. 13, 16. *Michigan Business Review,* Vol. XVIII, No. 4, July, 1966. Ann Arbor, Michigan: The University of Michigan.

Gaston, J. Frank, ed., *Patterns of Economic Growth,* p. 54. Prepared for the International Industrial Conference, San Francisco, September, 1965. New York: National Industrial Conference Board, Inc.

Johnson, Harry, M.D., "The Executive Asks the Doctor," p. 21. *Business Management,* September, 1966. Greenwich, Conn.: Management Magazines, Inc.

Krooss, Herman E., *American Economic Development,* pp. 359-360. Englewood Cliffs, N. J.: Prentice-Hall, Inc., © 1955.

"Leadership and Motivation," p. 48. *Conference Board Record,* Vol. III, No. 8, August, 1966. New York: National Industrial Conference Board, Inc.

"LTV Blitzes Its Way into Ranks of Giants," p. 179. *Business Week,* March 18, 1967. New York: McGraw-Hill, Inc.

Randall, Charles P., re-ed. 1964, "Education—An Investment in People," pp. 2-11. Washington, D. C.: Chamber of Commerce of the United States of America.

Sarnoff, General David, "Envisioning the Future," pp. 68-70. *Nation's Business,* © June, 1966. Washington, D. C.: Chamber of Commerce of the United States.

Shiskin, Julius, "Business Cycle Indicators: The Known and the Unknown," (n.d.), p. 9. Washington, D. C.: U. S. Department of Commerce, Bureau of the Census.

Sorcher, Dr. Melvin, "Motivating the Hourly Employee." *Behavioral Research Service,* 1967. Personnel and Industrial Relations Services, General Electric.

Spence, Clark C., *"The Sinews of American Capitalism,"* pp. 147, 164. New York: Hill & Wang, Inc., 1964.

Trabue, Bruce, ed., "It's Management's Turn to Listen," p. 3. *The Manager's Letter,* July 20, 1967. New York: American Management Association, Inc.

Wall Street Journal (Dallas), Aug. 8, 1966. George Shea: "The Outlook."

Wall Street Journal (Dallas), Mar. 6, 1967. Lee Berton: "Who Needs It?"

Wall Street Journal (Dallas), Mar. 28, 1967, p. 19. Frederick C. Klein: "You're the Boss."

Wall Street Journal (Dallas), Mar. 30, 1967. John Gray: "Notable & Quotable."

Walton, Eugene, "Communicating Down the Line: How They Really Get the Word," pp. 78-82. *Personnel*, July-August, 1959. New York: American Management Association, Inc.

Wichita Eagle, July 9, 1966, p. 4B. Sylvia Porter: "Your Money's Worth." Courtesy Wichita Eagle and Publishers-Hall Syndicate.

Wooldridge, Jack, ed., "Fringe Benefits—Now Rising Twice as Fast as Wages," pp. 50-52. *Nation's Business*, Vol. 54, No. 8, © August, 1966. Washington, D. C.: Chamber of Commerce of the United States.